Audrey Whiting

Born into a working-class family who did not own any books, Audrey Whiting started writing at six. Mostly little poems, stories and, at eight, a school play. Won 'the scholarship' at eleven and after leaving school took a secretarial course. Her first job was as a trainee cub reporter on the *Eastern Daily Press* for seven-and-six a week. Later she worked on newspapers abroad and spent three years in Italy.

GAL
AUDREY

AUDREY
WHITING

What are the roots that clutch?
T. S. Eliot

ARIEL BOOKS
BBC PUBLICATIONS

Dedicated to
Mother and Dad

The BBC Radio 4 serial based on this book was first broadcast in
Woman's Hour in 1986. It was abridged and produced by Pat
McLoughlin and read by Patience Tomlinson.

Published by BBC Publications
A division of BBC Enterprises Ltd
35 Marylebone High Street, London W1M 4AA

First published 1986
© Audrey Whiting 1986

ISBN 0 563 20465 6

Typeset in 10/11 Ehrhardt Linotron
by Wilmaset, Birkenhead
Printed in Great Britain by Cox and Wyman Ltd, Reading

Contents

Author's Note

I meant to write this book about myself, me, Gal Audrey. But Mother took over. She had a habit of that. She made me smile, at times. I think the reader will see what I mean.

Mother was a fighter. 'Things rankle with me,' she said, and the casualties piled up. Am I better, or worse, because of Mother? I don't know, others must judge. I survived because she forced me to. I'm glad I did. It has been great so far.

And though everything has changed, people don't. Not in Norfolk. I still rejoice to hear the old speech. Those characters of another time may never come again, but they still live for me.

1
Changelings

Mother didn't like us right from the start, because we were dark. 'I wish they'd been light, my kids,' she moaned, 'like *my* people.' But we were dark, my brother and I. We came out of the shadows. Creatures she didn't understand. It was like the gypsy's curse.

Yet after all we belonged to her. We would never belong to ourselves. She would make sure of that. All the women of mother's family claimed their own blood, however far and thinly spread. 'I do like light-'aired people,' she fretted, 'they allus look clean.' This made us ashamed. We were dark and unclean.

'His people, that's who yer like, you two. Nothin' like my people. No, that yer not.' She disclaimed us. Father's people were dark. Tarred with the same brush as we were. Mother didn't like them either. Deceitful, as well as dirty.

'I set my 'eart on them bein' fair.' She washed our hair in camomile lotion, packed in green envelopes. Washing-up water, it looked like. I was afraid it would blind me. It was a premonition. At seven, my teacher had to put me in front of the blackboard. I couldn't see from the back of the class. No one thought of testing my eyes. Not until I was ten. Then they put metal eyeglasses on me, that bit into my nose. I sobbed all by myself in front of the glass in Mum's bedroom; my beauty gone. 'It's yer own fault,' she snapped, 'you *would* read in bed, wun't you. So what dew you expect?'

Years later, I tasted camomile tea. It was good for female ailments, the chemist said. Like stewed undergrowth it was, bitter as the taste of my childhood.

But all mother's efforts made no difference. We were still dark, Dennis and I. We were a disappointment.

Besides that, we were shy. Mum didn't hold with that either. We hadn't turned out right. Not like *her* people. They could stick up for themselves. 'We were brought up to fear nothin',' she scowled, 'in our family.' We edged closer to each other for comfort. What went on in her mind was a mystery. She was a tower of strength that threatened to fall on top of us. If you bumped into her, she had sharp edges. We couldn't see her as she was; a fresh-faced countrywoman in a flowered pinafore, her blue eyes, child's eyes, round and wondering. Soft face, hard hands.

'I can't help it if I'm shy, Mum,' I snivelled.

'You dare tew answer me back! I'll clip your lug.'

Mother was a creature of habit. We studied her to avoid trouble. Fridays was the shampoo and a dose of syrup of figs. I hated the taste of it. It came up again. She slapped me hard and locked me in the coalhouse under the stairs. I blundered about on bits of coal, terrified of rats and spiders and ghosts. When she let me out I stood and blinked. I couldn't see, but I daren't say so. We were not on speaking terms.

'Kids,' she moaned, 'it don't pay to 'ave kids. I wish I'd never 'ad you two. I'd be 'appy now, 'stead a' mis'rable.' If she was really angry, she would bawl: 'I wish God had never sent me any children. I wish 'e would take you back.' Her body was racked with sobs, her face red and tear-stained.

Sometimes, out of revenge, we got up to our tricks. We plastered the furniture with jam while she was out shopping, pretending it was polish. She never forgave us for that.

Did I feel rejected when Mum said she didn't want us? They were just words. I ignored them. Either I was clever, or I just wanted to survive. She claimed I was clever and she was proud of me. 'That Gal Audrey learnt 'erself tew read at three. She were lyin' in bed with the chicken pox. I went up and she were readin' the *Evenin' News*.' She took the credit for my brains. They came from her side of the family. 'All our family was brainy,' she beamed, 'my brother Horrie could 'ave been a doctor, you know, if he'd a-stayed on at school.'

But it was plain she had made a mistake. Mother's brothers could wrestle and box. They won silver cups at the Lads' Club. They could fight, but they couldn't think. Poor Mum wasn't very gifted either. She depended on her instincts. But they were not very reliable.

I was no more than three when she sent me out for the fish and chips, across the main road in King Street. A motor-car smashed me down. I disappeared between the wheels. Against all the odds I was dragged out alive. Not even scratched.

'My stars! Did you see that? She went right under. It's a miracle she's alive.' A labourer picked me up tenderly and carried me into the fish shop like a doll.

'Put 'er up on the counter. See if she can speak,' the fish-shop-man said. The factory hands crowded in, sure I was dying. They stared in wonder at me. I squirmed on the marble counter. I felt cold and my dress was soaked. What would Mum say when she found out I had wet myself?

'This is all my 'usband's fault,' Mum bawled. She rushed into the shop, still in her apron, straight from the sink, her face bright red. I didn't dare to say anything, noticing how angry she was. ''E must 'ave 'is dinner on time. The minute 'e gits in from wark. Thaa's why I 'ad to send 'er out for it.' No one answered. After a few seconds, they drifted away. The excitement was over.

What we had for our dinner that day, I don't remember. But afterwards she took me to the doctor. 'I'm takin' you tew see Doctor Murphy,' she barked, 'so don't put y'r parts on.' She got out my old push-chair. The moths flew out of the pillow. She killed them at a blow and strapped me in. It felt all wrong. After all, I was a big girl now and push-chairs were for babies.

Dr Murphy was a Catholic, so he believed in miracles. 'Praise be to God, Mrs Emms!' He raised his hands and eyes heavenwards. 'Knocked down by a motor-car and nearly killed, yet not a mark on her little body!'

Mother simpered and pretended to be a nice kind person. The doctor didn't know what she was really like. Neither did the neighbours. She kept things dark, somehow. You have to live with people to know them. And we had to live with Mother. She pushed me home again at top speed and I settled down to play with my wooden bricks. They had kittens playing in the grass painted on them, rolling over, their paws in the air.

Whether Mum was peculiar to start with, or whether it came on later, I never knew. Or perhaps it was just being married to Father. ''Im, don't talk tew me about 'im and 'is ways. You'll never get tew the bottom of 'im. Sit there night after night be'ind that newspaper. Never say a blind word, 'e wun't.'

Dad was quiet and she was always nagging. He never knew which way she would fly. Before he sat down, she rushed out with a newspaper to spread over her cushion, so he wouldn't dirty it with his overalls. She made out he wasn't good enough for her. We got used to it. We never questioned what she did. We thought all mothers were the same. We didn't know she was a tyrant – not until later.

There were days when she was in a good mood and told me tales of the family. Perched on the arm of Dad's chair, I watched her face as she seemed to change into the people she was talking about.

'Before you was born,' she started, 'I mooched down a' Gentleman's Walk and into the Royal Arcade to look at the shops. It were that 'ot, an' I were right big wi' you.' She nodded, making her curlers rattle. 'But I couldn't sit still. I were that restless. All I wanted to dew was walk about. I were nearin' me time, yer see.'

Mum poked the fire and stared into it, going back five years. I listened quietly, though I'd heard it before.

'I 'ad that red coat on with the tippet an' I were reg'lar malted in it. I stopped outside a shop ter take it orf. Then I sees someone a-smilin' at me in the window. I couldn't make out who it were, 'cause it were closed. Then it struck me, it were a big doll. Its arms were stretched out to me. Its eyes were fixed on my face. I fear to be 'ipmetised. All the way 'oom I could see that doll in front of me. I say to yer father: "Charlie", I say, "I'm 'aunted."

' "Strike a light, Gladdy," 'e say. "You don't 'alf put the wind up me. Whatever dew you mean by that?"

' "I're seen a lovely doll in the Royal Arcade. Seem to be smilin' at me, jus' like a real person. I can't get it out a' my mind, an' thaa's a fack."

' "You want a good clear out," yer Dad say. 'E were takin' the rise out of me. 'E would a' course, bein' a man – or so 'e reckin ter be.'

Mum stood in front of the glass on the mantelpiece and started taking her curlers out. Big curls lay round her face like brown snails, doddermans, we called them. Then she smeared her Icilma vanishing cream all over her cheeks so they glistened in the firelight.

'Well, I wook up in the middle a' the night. I 'ad a terrible shock. That doll was standin' beside my bed! "Gladys", she say tew me, "you 'aven't got long to go, afore you 'ave your child. It'll be a little girl, an' it will 'ave a face jus' like mine." Wi' that she disappeared and I wook up streamin' with sweat. I thought my hour 'ad come.'

'Thaa's funny, Mum,' I said, 'was it a nightmare, or what?'

'Not ezackly,' she said, raking through the corkscrew curls with her big chromium comb. 'But that dream drew me back to the shop. Soon as ever I'd got me work done, I went to 'ave another look. There she were, large as life, in a bootiful pink dress, with long curly 'air an' a pink taffeta bow on top. I went straight in an' I ask, "'Ow much is that doll?" The woman say to me: "Oh no, maddim, that doll in't for sale. She's unly fer show. She're bin made specially fer royalty!" I were real disappointed. "Well, I unly ask," I say. "I in't got no money to throw in the street".'

Mum plonked her knickers on the fireguard to air. She was getting ready for the church social. I was going to do a turn on the stage for the Mothers' Guild. I was good at dancing and Mum had put me in a dancing troupe.

'Damn me,' she said, 'I still wanted to see that doll. I couldn't understand why. I made me way down to the Royal Arcade agin. But soon as I gits there I see the doll were gone. I were that upset. "Wherever's that bootiful doll gone?" I ask, nearly a-cryin' I were.

' "Why maddim, she've bin sold", the woman say to me.

' "Oh!" I say, "yer got a neck. You reckined she wun't fer sale, din't you?"

'She give me a funny look. "Well," she say, "I 'ad to break my word. We were orfered a large sum fer that doll, so we took it. It were some big lady wot bought it, lived out in India and were married to a Rah'jun."

'I went 'oom feelin' done out a-suffin'. Soon as ever I gets there me pains start. I shruck out to yer father: "Charlie," I shruck, "dew yew go an' git my mother 'ere, 'cause I'm done for."

'I'll never fergit wot I went threw bornin' yew.' Mum glared at me and flung a heap of black dust on the fire, covering the flames. The room grew dark and her face moody. 'I take on me oath,' she said, 'I were meant ter die, but they pulled me threw, Mrs Bland the midwife an' Dr Murphy 'atween 'em. I were on me last legs when they 'anded you over ter me in that bed. I took one look an' perked up. "My heart alive," I say, "this chile's zackly like that doll. My dream 'as come trew."

'Mrs Bland give me a look. She thought I were out a' me 'ead wi' that twilight sleep they give me. "Why yis, Mrs Emms," she say, "she's jus' like a little doll, in't she?"

'A-course, Mrs Bland din't know what I were talkin' about. An' I in't never let on ter a livin' soul, 'cept yer father.'

A tiny blue light flickered across the coal-dust, then it went off like a rocket and a yellow flame shot up, lighting the whole room. In that second I saw myself reflected in the big looking-glass on the wall; a doll in a pink frock, with a taffeta bow on top of her long curls.

'If yew sits there much longer in front a' that damn glass, I swear yer'll stick like that fer good,' Mum snapped, as she went on putting the finishing touches to my dress. Soon I would be ready to perform my dance at the church social: 'The Wedding of the Painted Doll'.

Everyone clapped and cheered when I did that turn. I stood inside a big box in the middle of the stage. When the curtains went up someone took the lid off the box and there I was. The audience all said, 'Ooh, look at that doll!' They didn't know I was a real girl, until I started dancing. Then I did a few jerky steps, stiff-legged with my arms stuck out in front.

Mum always got a vote of thanks from the vicar, or a bunch of daffs. It was only right she should; she was the one who made up the dance. But I never got anything myself. After all, I was only the one that danced it.

2
A Creaking Cart

'There's a lot a' goodness in cockles,' Mum said. She was boiling up a pailful, shells and all, on Grandma's stove in the back kitchen. I couldn't make out her expression through the steam, but she seemed to be licking her lips. Her petrol-blue toque was on wonky, her oatmeal swagger was slung on over her pinafore, for warmth. The kitchen was damp and cold. You could see the soles of people's feet, as they walked up and down on the iron grating in the ceiling. We were underneath the street.

'Gal Gladdy,' Grandma bawled down the stairs, ''ave yew got them damn cockles riddy yit?' Although Mum was married and had the two of us to look after, she was still expected to wait on Grandma as well. She was meant to be an invalid.

Mum screamed back. 'Hold yew hard, Mother, they 'aven't opened their eyes yit. Keep y'r wool on!'

'She's gittin' high-stirrical agin,' Mum whispered to me, 'that Boy Donny's bin workin' 'er up, ever since 'e went an' 'anged 'is 'at up wi' that young mawther a-down a' Goat Lane.'

Donny was Mother's youngest brother, born when Grandma was an old woman of forty-two. She'd never got over the shock to her system. She'd taken to her bed and depended on others to look after her.

'Trouble is,' Mum lifted out a cockle on her wooden spoon and glared at it, 'y'r Gran'ma depend on Donny. She might as well depend on a blade a' grass, fer all the blummin' good 'e is. Bin mollycollered all 'is life. 'E'll come a cropper one a' these days, yew mark my words.'

I kept a mournful face like Mum's. 'I dare say he will,' I said.

I knew that everyone in our family depended on someone else. They went to pieces when anyone died. They just lived off each other's blood till it was all sucked dry. Then they latched on to someone else to keep going.

'I'm blasted fed up wi' this job,' Mum grumbled. She bashed the cockles up and down with a wooden copper-stick like a truncheon. 'I in't 'ad a minute ter take me damn 'at orf, 'ave I?' She handed me the stick. 'Once them cockles 'ave got their eyes open, give us a shout.' With a look of sheer misery, she pointed up at the ceiling. 'I'm goin' up there to see to 'er.'

I dug down into the pail with my stick, but the cockles kept their eyes closed. They weren't ready yet, although a lovely savoury smell wafted up. It had brought the cat in.

'Git that blasted moggy out a' my way,' Mum spluttered, lashing out with her foot. There was no light on Grandma's stairs and the cat tripped Mum up. He ran away hissing and spitting. The brush and dustpan clattered down. They were kept on the stairs.

'Whatever's a-goin' on, Gal Gladdy?' Grandma jumped out of bed and stood on the landing in her calico nightgown. Her eyes were so bright and angry they seemed to light up the stairs.

'Git yew back ter kip, Mother, that in't nothin' unly that blummin' cat,' Mum called. 'I'm bringin' yew up a round a' toost ter be gittin' on with.'

The toast lay on the brick floor. Mum foraged for it, wiped it on the corner of her apron and put it back on the plate. 'Take that up tew yer Nan, Gal Audrey. I'll look arter them cockles.' I handed her the stick.

Grandma lay in her four-poster frowning. Her hair was matted, her skin crumpled and yellow. The curtain was pulled against the light. It was four o'clock on a spring afternoon, but there was no sun in that room. Grandma didn't believe in the sun. She was propped up on pillows of striped ticking without any slips on, because the washing hadn't been done. A funny smell came out of her big aspidistra on the wickerwork table by the bed. She stared at the toast in disappointment.

'I were lookin' forward ter them cockles,' she complained, 'thaa's your Mother all over, she never could do nothin' right. She were an 'alf-hour late a-gittin' 'ere, an' all.'

'Well, you see, Nan,' I explained, 'she 'ad to meet us out a' school. Then it's a rare long way up Mariner's Lane to get 'ere.'

She gave me an aggrieved look. 'If the truth be known, y'r Mother unly come 'ere ter git a good tea. She know full well y'r Grandad allus bring cockles 'oom on a Weddensd'y.'

Grandad was an engine-driver on the Great Eastern, between Norwich Thorpe and Yarmouth Vauxhall. He always took a pailful of beer with him. They drank it between them, him and the fireman, it was that hot in the cab as they shovelled the coals into the furnace. Then they filled up the empty pail with cockles down at the wharf and brought them home for tea.

Grandma punched the pillows viciously. For an invalid she was full of energy. She had big muscles on her arms as well. ''And me my teeth, will yer.' I gave her the old cup without any handle.

'That toast is nice and soft, don't you worry, Nan.'

'Let's 'ope so,' she frowned, 'these teeth in't up ter much now. Specially when it come ter things like toast.' She put them in and I heard them click. After that, I could understand what she said better. 'She in't put marge on this toast, 'as she?'

'Oh no, Nanny,' I said quickly to avoid arguments, 'it's best butter, like yew always has.'

I daren't upset Grandma, she ruled the roost. The whole family took turns to wait on her in that bed. Mum, Auntie Renee, Auntie Eunie. The men never did a hand's turn, because they were men, and no one expected it. But if people didn't do what Grandma wanted, she had a heart attack.

'Your Mother's a creakin' cart an' yew lot give in to 'er,' Dad always said. 'She'll never die of a weak 'eart, yew see if she don't. She'll outlive the lot on us.' He was right. She outlived him in the end. And though Grandma depended on Uncle Donny, it was him that went to pieces when she died. They had to cart him off to Hellesdon Infirmary.

'Git my cuu'm orf a' that mantelpiece, Gal Audrey.' Why ever she had to do her hair before she ate the cockles was a puzzler. I searched behind the tall glass case with the blue bird inside. He had a sharp beak and sat on a twig, doubled up with song. But you couldn't hear it because he was stuffed. I found the big steel comb. It was full of grey hairs, stiff and wiry like dog's hairs. 'Y'r on the moult, Nan,' I said, cleaning the comb.

Mum chased up the stairs with a pudding basin full of cockles, the shells chinking. She still had her hat on wonky. She glared accusingly at Grandma. 'I see y'r done y'r 'air,' she puffed.

Grandma sighed. 'If I wait fer yew ter dew it, I'll be 'ere till next week, wun't I?'

'Silly ole fossil,' Mum said, under her breath, 'she'll be 'ere come what may.'

Grandma had been brought up with a skivvy to wait on her. That was her trouble. Her father had kept a draper's shop till he went bust, then the whole family landed up in the workhouse. That was how she'd married Grandad; just to get out of it.

'Where's the blasted pepper then?' she moaned.

'My stars! I fergot all about the pepper.' Mum drew her lips in.

'Buck yew up, Gal Gladdy.' Grandma chided.

'Thaa's no good yew talkin' like that,' Mum snorted, 'I'm breakin' in a new pair a' corsets, an' I can't move in 'em.'

Grandma took no notice. She shook the basin hard and the cockles dropped neatly out of their shells on to her plate in little squelchy piles. They were plump and white, with dainty orange frills. My mouth watered at the sight. 'Come yew on, my little maid,' Grandma crooned, in a good mood now, 'yew jest 'ave a taste a' these, that'll set yew up.' I popped a juicy one into my mouth before she changed her mind. 'Will yew go and git y'r pore ole Nan the winnegar?' she whined.

'Right y'are, Nan.'

I ran down to the kitchen to keep her in a good mood. 'That's the ticket, my sugar.'

The gramophone was going. Someone had wound it up. It was playing 'Ain't it grand to be bloomin' well dead'. Uncle Donny was sitting in front of a steaming plate of cockles. He'd got all my cigarette cards spread out on the table and Mum's *Titbits* as well. His cap was pushed to the back of his head and he had a wedge of bread in his fist.

''Ello, Gal Audrey,' he leered at me, his blue eyes protruding, 'where'd yew spring from?' He slurped as he gobbled the cockles down. I was afraid of him, even though he was my uncle. He always tried to pet me.

'Nan want the vinegar.' I put my hand out and Uncle Donny pulled me on to his lap. He fondled my hair with his greasy fingers. His breath smelt of beer.

Mum snatched his cockles and poured them all down the sink. He let out a roar and I was free. I slid down underneath the table.

'Wot the p'liceman,' he bawled, 'gi'mme back my cockles!'

'I'll gi' yer a fist in the jaw, if yer like. Comin' in 'ere, stinkin' a' booze suffin' pewtrid. Yew c'n sling y'r 'ook.'

I scuttled out of the way. When I got back to Nan with the vinegar bottle, she was wiping her lips on the corner of the counterpane. 'I're finished now. Yew c'n take the vinegar back an' wash the basin up. An' put me teeth back.' I handed her the cup. It was full of bits of food floating about. She dropped her teeth in it with a splash and settled back, eyes closed. 'I think I may be taken bad,' she groaned. 'Where's my Boy Donny? Why doan' 'e come 'oom? I'm all on thorns when 'e's out.' She looked as gloomy as her aspidistra.

''E is 'oom, Nan,' I said, ''e's in the kitchen 'avin' 'is cockles. 'E ask to borrer a shillin' orf a' Mum, but she in't got it.'

Grandma didn't answer. Her lips were pale and very thin. I crept downstairs, tiptoeing. 'She's asleep,' I told Mum. 'Or she's a-sulkin'.'

'Thaa's more like it,' Mum said, 'fer somebody wi' nothin' ter dew all day, she can't 'alf gorge. She're et the 'ole lot wot I took up. I reckin she're got a tapeworm. Yew never know y'r got one till it gits up inter y'r throat, then yew know all about it, 'cause that's when yew gits stifled.'

''Ave I got one a' them, Mum?' I asked, frightened.

'Certainly not!' she snapped. 'I wun't allow that.'

Uncle Donny had gone off on his bike. I sat down to my plate at last. Steam dripped down the walls and the sink was blocked up with shells. 'My stars,' Mum said, 'that Boy Donny in't 'alf a spoofer, askin' ter borrer money orf a' me on a Weddensdy. Said 'e were skint. I told 'im to go an' ask 'is young mawther for it, if she in't ditched 'im be now. 'Er father keep that Marcantonio's fish shop. She's an Eyetie, y'know.'

'An Eyetie? What's that, Mum?'

'Eyeties? Why, they're the next worst thing to a diddicoy. Crafty an' cunnin' they are. Can't trust none on 'em. Saller faces and sloe eyes, they a' got. Stick a knife in yer, soon's look at yer. 'Ot tempered, like all them Cath'lics. Murder one another, they does. That Boy Donny'll git 'is just desserts. 'E went an' pinched me engagement ring an' pawned it down a' Bridewell Alley. I never did git it back. 'E's full a' them tricks.'

A quavering voice interrupted Mum's conversation. 'Can yer come up 'ere, Gal Gladdy, I don't feel nonc too cracky. Where's them Glauber Salts?'

''Strewth,' Mum ground her teeth, 'she can't let us alone two minutes, can she? 'Ere y'are, take 'em up.' I balanced a cup of water and the Glauber Salts on a plate.

'What's the matter, Nan?'

'I 'eard that blummin' dawg 'owlin' next door, thaa's a sure sign of a death,' Grandma said bitterly, as the salts fizzed in the cup. 'I can't keep nothin' down, unly slops. I're got proud flesh all over me body, an' that doan' 'alf smart. I reckin I'm a gonner, Gal Audrey.' Tears squeezed from the corners of her eyes.

'Don't worry, Nan, we'll look after you. Drink your medicine.' I felt sorry for her then.

'No one don't seem ter realise I're seen Queen Victoria in the flesh,' she whimpered. She drank down the salts in one gulp and shuddered.

I made myself comfortable beside her on the bed. 'Oh Nan, tell us all about it,' I said. I'd heard it all before, but I didn't mind hearing it again.

We all realised Mum couldn't stomach too much of Grandma, but the one she really hated was Dad's mother. There was always a row about going to tea there on a Sunday.

'I'm not allowed to dew what I like of a Sunday. No, certainly not! I're got ter turn round an' go down a-Cinder Oven Row ter please your ole mother, 'aven't I?' Mum was laying the law down again. She ended up smashing two plates.

'It's your Father,' she bawled, "e make my narves suffin' bad, 'e dew.' Dad got down on his knees and picked up the pieces. Mum emptied a kettle of water into a bowl, her bare arms bulging out of her pink petticoat. 'I'll 'ave to 'ave a sluice down afore I go,' she shouted, 'so you'll 'ave ter wait. Whatever 'ave yew done wi' that soap?'

The cloudy water showed where it had gone. 'It's in the bowl, Mum.' I went outside to fish for the flannel. It had gone down the plug-hole and lay in the drain. I handed it to her and she ducked her head to wash her neck, then dabbed angrily at her nose and chin. 'It make me shudder ter think a' that ole beggar. 'Er lies and 'er wicked tongue 'as nearly put paid ter this 'oom more'n once.'

I did up the buttons on my brother's raincoat and put my sou'-wester over my curls. Mum went upstairs in her petticoat and came down again in her powder-blue grosgrain and a jockey cap to match. Dad hid under his trilby and made a performance of locking up, which we hardly ever did.

'That ole cat don't deserve a good daughter-in-law like me,' Mum scowled at Dad, as we set off down the hill. Dad's face was set, as though dreading what was to come.

Dennis and I walked on in front, scared in case people heard Mum talking so loud in the middle of the street. The children called to us from the swing-fields; we longed to play, but we were going out to tea.

Not far from the River Wensum were six little cottages all joined together, with paved backyards and a wash-house between them. Grandma's was the first one. They all smelt mouldy when you went in because they often got flooded when the river rose.

My Granny Emms was always cheerful, not like our other granny, who was always piping her eye. When we arrived she was singing in her wash-house: 'Cockles and mussels, alive, alive oh!' Hearing the gate slam, she ran out to meet us.

'She're 'ad a drop,' Mum whispered.

'Shut yew up!' Dad warned.

Granny's face lighted up as she bent to kiss us. She had a big head of curly dark hair, narrow shoulders and wide hips in a flowered pinafore. It was her best one for Sunday. Her lips felt like blotting paper. She had lost most of her teeth and her new ones pained her, so she never wore them. Dad hung back when his mother attempted to kiss him. Mum didn't want him to kiss her back. She didn't hold with 'show'.

'Come yew on in out a' the cold, an' 'ave one a' my buns, you two.' Granny held on to our hands, pulling us indoors. 'I know you're bin good children today.' She opened her drawer and got out the rag doll for me to nurse. Mother frowned. She thought Granny was two-faced and ran us all down behind our backs.

Grandad sat in his old flock armchair fast asleep under the *News of the World*. He was bolt upright with his arms folded. He'd kicked his boots off and his short, bowed legs hardly reached the floor. His mouth hung open and his face was clammy. A fire flickered in the grate, but the room was chilly and stuffy at the same time. Grandad's clay pipe lay on the arm of his chair. It had a dog with sharp teeth carved on the bowl. There were two white china spaniels with long ears on the mantelpiece staring down at me.

'I'll soon rouse that fire up,' Granny clucked, poking at the cinders. The brick floor was stained with red ochre. It came off on the piece mats. They were made of strips of rag knotted on to sackcloth. Only the poorest of the poor had mats like that, Mum always said. Dennis and I sat down on the shiny horsehair sofa and gradually slid off again. No one noticed. Mother was intent on the custard tarts waiting on the sideboard. The sight cheered her up.

'Yew in't bin a-bakin' agin, 'ave yew, Mother?' She was all smarmy.

'Yis, but they 'aven't riz the way they ought, Gladys.' Granny handed the plate round.

'It's that oven, I reckin,' Mum soothed. I knew she was thinking what a rotten cook Granny was and how Father never had a good inside lining and ailed a lot when he was first married. Grandad woke up, focusing slowly on us.

'Come on, master,' Granny chided, 'stir y'r stumps.'

'I were considerin' goin' down the dyke,' Grandad yawned, and did his collar up. We brightened up. He might take us for a row in his dinghy. Grandad's family had been fishermen at Yarmouth. At weekends he still went out with his bread and cheese; his pocket stuffed with flies on hooks.

Grandad caught butterflies down the backwater. He collected them in glass cases on the living-room wall. Their wings were the only bright things in the whole house; everything was dark oak or mahogany. The walls were papered bottle green. The prize specimen in the collection was a monster of a stag-beetle, with antlers on its head like two blades of a saw. Grandad took it down to show us again.

''E's a rummun, in't 'e?' he chuckled. I stared into its strange face. It had eyes a bit like grandfather's.

'Whatever's wrong wi' that child?' Grandma burst out. 'She don't 'alf look white!'

'Anaemy-ic,' Mother snorted. 'She don't eat nothin', thaa's 'er trouble.'

'Same thing wot took my poor little Malcolm orf. 'E would a' bin alive terday. He shrank ter nothin'. Pernicious, it were. Nothin' they could dew. 'Ave yew tried that Parrish's Food?'

I shuffled my feet, then roamed round the room.

'Radio Malt,' Mother snapped, 'thaa's what they recommend in my doctor's book. But she wun't swaller it. It's sheer badness.'

'Yew may lose 'er then, Gladys,' Granny whispered, so I shouldn't hear. 'Will yew 'ave a custard, my beauty?' Her eyes were full of tears. I couldn't understand why. I didn't like her custard tarts much, they were too runny. I took one and kept it to give my brother.

Grandad was squashing his bunions into his hob-nailed boots moaning. Everything he did was slow and deliberate, like Father. ''E want a dose a' Kruschens down a' 'im,' Mum always said. She hated languid people.

'Yew never want to git old like me, Gal Audrey,' he sighed. He put on his clothes one by one, a pullover, a waistcoat, then his jacket and overcoat, a striped scarf, knitted mittens and a big check cap. He turned into a fat man, looking sideways at his profile in the glass.

'Yew want to wrap up, Sam, it's perishin'.' Granny clicked her tongue as she lit the oil-lamp in the middle of the table. ''E's bronickle, y'know, Gladys.' She nodded her big head up and down.

Mum's face flushed. I knew the mention of bronchitis meant one thing to her. Consumption! Mum claimed that Dad had married her under false pretences, knowing he had consumption in the family. She'd been 'decoyed' into a family of invalids. She couldn't forgive them.

Grandad stomped out. 'Fare ye well, tergether.' We scurried after him, coats and scarves flying in the wind, ready for any excitement that might come our way.

After tea, Granny read the teacups. Mine as well. A teacup was her book, Mum said. 'Looks to me like yew'll all be goin' to Gorleston this year. There's a "G" in your cup, plain as anything.' Granny's eyes were dark and strange, as she studied the future.

'I'll 'ave to warn yew about the lodgin's though. They don't look none too clean, accordin' to the cup.'

'Come on 'ere. We're 'ad enough a' this for'chun tellin',' Grandad barked. He didn't hold with it. Just then the door opened and Auntie Jessie, Dad's sister, walked in, followed by Uncle Will and our two cousins, Sheila and Maurice. Mum's face clouded over. She got up quickly.

'Git y'r clo'es on, yew two. We're goin' 'oom.' I knew why. It was Mum's jealousy. She didn't like Dad mixing with his sister Jessie. They were too close for her liking.

Dad was teasing Cousin Maurice, chucking him under the chin and pulling his hair. Mum couldn't allow that. He looked up and saw her frowning and scrambled to his feet. By this time, Mum was out of the house.

Father came panting behind, one arm in his coat sleeve and his trilby on backwards. 'Whatever's the matter with yew?' he shouted. 'I never even finished my tea.'

'Your tea!' she stormed, 'yew 'ad plenty a' time ter play wi' that Boy Maurice, din't yer? Yit yew ignored your own kids, din't yer? Thaa's yew all over – other people's kids is more ter yew than your own flesh an' blood. These poor children know all about yew.'

'Yew've always got somethin' ter crab about,' Dad muttered.

Mother charged along like a mad bull. I was sorry she made us leave, because I was half in love with Cousin Maurice. He had black fluffy curls at the front and cupid's-bow lips. I couldn't wait for next Sunday. I considered pinching some of Mum's home-made toffee out of the tin to give him. 'Let's go out on the swings,' I whispered to my brother. We crept out of the back door and left Mum and Dad to get on with their row.

3
An Occasion in the Family

Auntie Renee and Uncle Sid had just waved goodbye and gone off to Yarmouth, on their honeymoon. The house felt cold without them; as though they'd taken all the warmth with them.

'I'll make a pot a' tea,' Mum sniffed. She'd just been piping her eye. My brother dried his eyes on the sleeve of his sailor suit. A minute ago he was hanging on to Auntie, shouting: 'I want to go on the "moon" as well!' He loved her because she was pretty and smelt nice. She pampered him too, which was more than Mum did. On Sundays she bought him a cornet from Marcantonio's, half pink and half white. Mum had managed to pull him off her sister, without spoiling the pink silk going-away costume she wore.

The whole family were gathered in our house for the wedding. It was times like these that Auntie Eunie brought out the caul. She'd been born with it over her face and her body. Now she kept it in a box and sprinkled it with talcum. 'It's ter keep it dry, dew it might perish.' She took the lid off, her face working. The tip of her tongue darted out and in. It was forked, like a snake's.

The caul was handed round from one to the other in silence. Everyone had a good look at it and passed it on. While the caul went round, we munched pickled onions and potted meat sandwiches.

All the time she was chewing, Auntie Eunie kept on jawing. She had a big white hat with a wired brim pulled down over her eyes. It was the fashion. 'Thaa's a good luck charm, that is,' she gloated. 'I're kep' it all me life. When I were fu'st born, they all say – strike a light, whatever is it? They couldn't see me prop'ly, 'cause the caul was all over me, right over me 'ead, like a second skin. Dead white, it were too. There weren't 'alf a commotion.'

We weighed up what Auntie said; all sitting in a row on a form, because there weren't enough chairs. I was squashed up against Auntie Beattie who was nicknamed 'Tank' because she had such a big body. Uncle Ernie, with the shrapnel in his brain, was wedged on the other side. Ruby and Tom, my two sandy-haired cousins, were trying to lynch each other under the table, making it lurch from side to side and rattling the cups. Auntie Beattie kicked them hard to keep them quiet.

Grandma kept her smelling salts to her nose and sobbed about losing her poor little girl Renee, as though she had died. Grandad took no notice. He was asleep, with his mouth sagging and little bits of spit dribbling out of the corners.

Uncle Donny was dressed far too young, in a velvet page-boy's outfit, his fair hair hanging over the wide collar. His pockets were bulging with Mum's Maids of Honour. Dad dodged out of his way when he came closer. 'I can't stick that Donny,' he frowned. Dad hated him because Donny was always put on pozzy when Dad was courting Mum in the front-room, before they got married. He hid behind the sofa and reported them to Grandma. Then Mum got it! Dad had to pay him to go out; that was why Dad always called him Judas.

Uncle Bertie, the champion lightweight, was trying to get in between Auntie Hetty and Uncle Joe. Auntie Hetty was Dad's sister. Mum said she was a real frump with her hair in a bun, at her age. Every time she looked at Uncle Bertie he let out a whinny like a horse. He'd been bashed on the nose so often it had affected his sinus tubes, Mum said. His face was a sight and the girls didn't like him. Auntie Hetty sat making eyes at her brother-in-law, Uncle George, the poacher. Mum liked him best. He often copped a rabbit for us. And when Mum was a little nipper, Uncle George had bought her a doll with his first week's wages. Mum still remembered the joy of it. A doll of her very own. The only doll she ever had.

Auntie Eunie's eyes gleamed like someone gone barmy when she looked at the caul. But no one seemed to notice it, except Dad and I. They were all peculiar in that family.

'Essentric,' Dad said, under his breath. He didn't intend to say too much. After all, Auntie Eunie was Mother's flesh and blood. Mum looked all right, decked out in her canary voile and the gunmetal shoes with Cuban heels. She'd made a big kiss-curl in the front, but she spoilt herself by sliding her plate about with her tongue, trying to dislodge the crumbs that got in there.

'They 'ad ter pull it orf a' me 'ead right quick, lest I would a' bin sufficated,' Auntie drooled on. 'Mind yew, I were perfick underneath, like a little doll, I were.'

Pity the doll had turned into Auntie, with those warts and the hairs sticking out of them. Mum said she was full of spite. She ran you down behind your back and she had a name for being tight-fisted. 'Yew'll never git that Eunie ter part wi' nothin'. Blast! She even begrudge 'er own shit!'

'Mother were orfered a rare lot a' money fer that caul.' Auntie gave a weird smile. 'But she wun't take it. "Oh no", she say, "s'long's that Gal Eunie keep that, she'll keep 'er luck. If she ever lose it, 'er luck'll go."

'I in't never lawst it,' Auntie nodded her head in triumph. 'There's some as can work magic with cauls, an' put the tizzy on ter people wot they don't like. They got sartin' powers, cauls 'as. There's fishermen down a-Yarmouth way, wot wun't put out ter sea, lest they 'ave one a' them in their pocket.'

Just then Mum brought in the seed cake and lemon curd tarts. In the rush to get one, Auntie dropped the box and the caul fell out. It made a little thumping noise as it hit the floor. It lay there on the coconut matting, dry and grey, like an old dead spider, or a ball of Granny's combings. No one dared touch it. They all seemed to cower away from it.

Auntie was the centre of attention as she bent down and picked it up carefully. She held it out in the palm of her hand. The caul gradually turned itself over, with a crackling sound, like a little sigh. It made you feel funny to see it, as though it might jump at you. But it was only Auntie's old tricks. Some of the family had seen it before. But my brother was only little and he didn't realise.

'Look at that!' he shrieked, white as a sheet. 'That fear ter be a-comin' ter life!'

'My stars!' Auntie cackled, enjoying herself. 'Yer see that. It in't dead yit. That'll go on livin' 's'long as I dew, an' thaa's a fack. When I peg out, that'll die wi' me. Speaks fer itself.

'I warn yer,' she croaked at the family, 'if anyone try an' pinch it orf a' me, I sh'll know, 'cos that'll give me a shout.'

'Mangy ole thing,' my brother yelled out.

Auntie turned on him and slapped him full in the face. He screamed and held his cheek, where the marks of her hand showed up bright red.

Mum flew at her sister like a tiger. 'Hold yew hard!' she bawled, spit coming out of her mouth. 'What dew yew mean by layin' inter that child like that? 'E in't dewin' yew no 'arm. Yew always was a spiteful bitch! Yew c'n git out a' my 'ouse, quick as yew like, or I'll fist yew one in the snout!'

Dennis was bawling his head off, making the most of it. He hardly ever got any sympathy. 'Stop that blarring, son,' Dad said gruffly.

Mum rounded on Dad then. 'Pore little kid,' she spluttered,

'yew in't got no sympathy fer yore own flesh an' blood, 'ave yew? Callous is what yew are. Call yoreself a father! Come 'ere, my sugar.' She put both great arms round Dennis's head, trapping him against her chest. He couldn't breathe properly and all I could hear was a muffled bleating coming out of Mother's frock.

Auntie jumped up and burst out crying. 'She's ordered us out, me own sister! Would yew credit that? I don't know what ter make on it. She's nothin' but a turncoat!'

Uncle Ted got up and tried to calm his wife down. He was a sensible man, so Dad said. His new plus-fours were covered in beer and he swayed a bit. ''Strewth!' he stuttered in a slurred voice, 'shut yew up, Eunie. Gladdy din't mean nothin' by it. Don't yew be ser mur-hearted. I'm not a-goin' yit. I in't even finished my drop a' stout.'

Auntie gave him a shove with her elbow and he fell against the door. 'What dew yew know about it,' she snapped, ''oo ask yew ter open yore trap? She's my sister, not yours.' She stopped crying, though her face reminded me of the red cabbage Dad chopped up for pickling at Christmas. She grabbed the caul from the place where she'd hidden it; underneath her hat on the chiffonier. She crammed the hat on her head and made for the back door.

'I'm buggered if I'll be dictated tew by sich as yew. I know when I'm not wanted. It'll be a long time afore I darken these doors agin. I were just orf any'ow. Yew could a-waited afore yew got ser on-civil. Ted's got ter be up fer ha'-past four in the mornin'. We can't lay an' stink like some can. So we'll allie!'

Clutching the caul, Auntie took herself off with Uncle following behind. At the last minute, Mum gave in and put two short cakes in a brown paper bag. 'That'll dew fer yore lunch, Ted,' she wheedled, pushing them into his hands.

'Come yew on indoors,' Dad barked, 'thaa's a-thunderin' out there, an' like to rain.'

Mum shut the back door and put some more coal on the fire. ''Er an' that caul,' she said, 'she will cart that out when there's an occasion in the family, an' it always cause trouble, don't it? Yew'd think there wus a cuss on it.' She ran the steel comb through her hair and put the kiss-curl back, singing 'Don't Go Down In the Mine, Dad, Dreams very often come true . . .' It was her favourite. The others joined in at the tops of their voices. We were all cheerful again.

There was a pailful of cockles boiling in their shells and we had plenty of beer left.

'Which Auntie May is this one, Mum?' I held up the photograph of a cheeky face with a black fringe. She was wearing a clown's pointed hat with white bobbles down the front. Mum grabbed the photo, glared at it, then at me.

'Yew mean ter say yew forgot, Gal Audrey? Why, she's the one wot danced on the 'Ippodrome. She in't that poor one that got burnt up. No, not be a long chalk.' Mum piled the coal on the living-room fire, damping down the flames.

'Yer gittin' them two mixed up, aren't yer? Course, they was both called May, I know. But one of 'em was me own sister and the other May was me mother's sister. There was a big difference atween 'em.'

'However did that other one come ter get burnt up then, Mum?' I asked. The flames shot up, crackling and dancing.

Mum wiped her eyes on her calico apron and sniffed. 'My heart alive, it were terrible. She were only three-year-old an' all. She 'ad the croup, yer see, an' she kep' 'em all awake. So me mother give 'er a dose a' loddanum ter keep 'er quiet. Then she tiptoed downstairs an' left 'er fast asleep. Course, she went an' forgot all about the candle wot stood next to 'er bed. She 'ad six other kids ter see to.'

Mother blew her nose with a loud crack. 'There was one 'orrible shriek and me mother rushed ter the bottom a' the stairs. There stood 'er pore little May at the top, covered in flames. 'Er nightgown was set fire to, even 'er lovely long 'air was all lit up an' burnin'. It lay in black cinders all round 'er pore little 'ead when she were in 'er coffin. She was 'oldin' a bootiful wax doll in 'er arms an' it 'ad all melted away, unly the shoes was left, 'cause they was made out a' gunmetal, yer see.

'It don't bear thinkin' about. It brook yore pore grandma's 'eart, that did. She never got over it. "Gladdy", she say ter me, "I'll always see that dear child's face an' smell 'er burnin' till my dyin' day." The shock on it brought on 'er dropsy. 'Er body got ser big she couldn't git about no more. They 'ad ter git 'er a truss. But she wun't wear it. That obstinitt she're always bin, my ole woman.

'The results on it were she wouldn't never go out no more. She jus' stopped in 'er 'ouse. The whool thing affected 'er 'eart. They never knew when she might fall down dead. But a' course, that Dr Flack, 'e say ter me, "Yore mother'll never die of 'eart failure, yew see if she don't. Why, 'er 'eart's a lot stronger'n mine." '

I put the photograph carefully back in the old wooden cigar box. 'But what about the other one, Mum? The Auntie May that went on the stage?'

'Now, she come orf better,' Mum brightened up, 'she died out in India.'

'She died? What, that one an' all? 'Owever did she get out in India, Mum?'

'On a big boat, all the way ter New Jelly.'

'New Jelly, that sounds a nice place.' I put my spoon down hoping Mum wouldn't notice.

'Eat that arrer-root up, Gal Audrey,' she snapped, 'yew in't even touched it yit.' I forced it down, gagging. It was like slimy frog spawn. I had to have it because I was delicate.

'But why's she got that pointed 'at on, Mum?'

'She used ter sing a song in that 'at, like Florrie Forde.

I alwu'us 'old wi' 'avin' it, if yer fancy it.
'Cause a little a' wot yew fancy does yew good.'

Mum lolloped round the living-room, barging into the furniture, flinging her fat legs up in the air. Dad snorted in disgust. 'Oh dear, oh law, she were a client!' Mum flopped down gasping. 'So, I were tellin' yer, wun't I? That were 'ow she met that Indian. 'E made 'isself known tew 'er after 'er act.' Mum patted her hair in the mantelpiece mirror and smoothed her eyebrows.

'Indian, what Indian?'

'Why, the one 'oo took 'er ter New Jelly, a' course. 'E fell in love wi' 'er. 'E took a fancy tew 'er feet. They were that dainty, yer see. Indians like that sort a' thing. Tiny feet.'

'Oo-er, Mum!' I giggled. 'I thought that was the Chinese.'

'Contradictin' agin, Gal Audrey. I'm tellin' yer 'e was a' Indian, black as jet and dressed up in a turbine. Trouble was, once 'e got 'er on that boat she was took seasick an' confined tew 'er cabin. She unly come out when he promised ter marry 'er. It wun't a' done fer 'er ter spew up on 'er weddin' day, now would it? She soon got over 'er little indisposition.'

Mum washed up my arrowroot basin and wiped it on her apron. Then she blew her nose and dabbed her eyes. 'Soon's ever they got there, 'e give 'er an elefrunt.'

'An elephant, whatever for?'

'Fer a weddin' present, a' course. They all 'ave elefrunts personally out there. Yer Auntie May uster sit on top of its 'ead in a sort a' contraption called a how-d'ye-dew.'

Dad was shaking with laughter behind his newspaper. 'Whatever are yew a-golderin' at, Charlie?' Mum barked suspiciously.

'Jus' suffin' wot's in this paper,' Dad said, pulling his face straight.

'Trouble were she couldn't settle down. She kep' on writin' letters 'oom. Yer Grandma writ straight back an' told 'er ter sit tight where she was. Next thing we 'eard, they'd fell out, 'er an' 'im.'

'Oh Mum, did they hurt theirselves?'

'Waddya mean,' Mum snapped, 'yew in't bin listening ter wot I say, 'ave yew?'

'I was listening, Mum, but yew said they fell out of the how-d'ye-dew.'

'I din't mean that, did I? I meant they fell out with each other,' Mum snorted. 'Well, me Auntie May, she say she wun't goin' tew 'ave no one a-sittin' on 'er, so she give 'im the push. Said she were fed up wi' drinkin' sherbert all day long and a-playin' snakes an' ladders. Yer see, all them wives 'as ter be locked in a harum, wi' iron bars acrawse the winders. That were when the letters stopped,' Mum's face was solemn. 'Yer pore Grandma she say: "Whatever's 'appened ter me pore Sister May? She in't writ an' I keep on a-worrittin' about 'er."

'Yer Grandad 'e say: "That Indian might a' done 'er in, if I was yew I'd see inter it."

'Yer pore Grandma, she put 'er best 'at on and she went down a' the Town 'All an' reported it. Course she never went out, unly in emargencies, and that were one. Them lot down a' the Town 'All, they writ orf ter the British Console, Lord Fancy Tart it were.'

'Vansittart,' Dad interrupted, though he didn't seem to be listening.

'Thaa's wot I say,' Mum quacked. 'Well, they got a letter back in a big black envelope. Said as 'ow she'd passed away in Jelly 'Orspital. Yer Grandma wun't 'alf done. "Me very own sister," she sobbed, "wot always made us laugh with 'er songs an' 'ad sich lovely feet, she's gorn ferever." '

'Is that all?' I said.

'All? Wot more d'ye want? 'Cept nobody in the family's ever bin called May since then. They was both onlucky, yer see. Them as gits named May never makes old buuns. It's like them ole tales they uster tell when I were little.'

'What tales, Mum?'

'Why, they uster say as 'ow the may were a sign a' the spring a-comin', but yew dussn't pluck it, nor bring it in the 'ouse, dew it would be sure ter draw someone underground with it when it died.

'Ter think she'd a' bin forty-eight be now and an ole woman like y'r Gran'ma, if she'd a' lived. She were that dainty. Allus dressed in white like the flowers. A lovely face she 'ad, sparklin' eyes. People uster turn round in the street ter look at 'er.'

I studied the pudgy cheeks, the black beauty spot and the protruding teeth. She wasn't really pretty like my paper fairy in the Pop-Up Scenes book. In fact, she was exactly like Mum. But no one turned round to look at her twice, not so's you'd notice.

4
Living for Pleasure

'She's going to be clever, Mrs Emms,' my headmistress told Mother. 'She's very grown-up for three, you know. Your Audrey's the best one in the Infants.'

Mother smirked as she and Miss Olorenshaw stared down at me. They seemed to be asking me to do something. I couldn't tell what. But it made me uneasy.

'Take after my family, she do,' Mother was smug. 'I're got brothers wot 'ave won cups, y'know.' She didn't say it was for boxing down at the Lads' Club.

'Why Mrs Emms, you might even make a teacher out of Audrey.'

Mother clucked like a hen who had laid a very large egg. 'Fancy that.'

Father's face clouded when he was told. 'I don't like the sound er that,' he grunted. 'Why, she'd 'ave to stop on at school till she was sixteen. You know such as us can't afford them capers. We're unly working people.'

'Yew don't 'alf gi' me the 'ump,' Mum snapped. 'I've always 'ad it in mind fer Gal Audrey ter be clever, in't I? It's in 'er, in't it? An' yew can't put it where it in't, can yew? 'Sides, waddya think I bought 'er that inkwell with the 'elmit on top for, when she were christened?'

Dad couldn't deny that. A funny present for a new-born babe, he'd thought so at the time. But he hadn't realised what it was leading to; a threat.

But infants' school led to ailments, scarlet fever, whooping cough, chicken pox, then measles. 'That Gal Audrey don't 'alf ail a lot,' Mum moaned. The chicken pox lasted weeks and left me with two marks in my forehead. I lay alone in the bedroom I shared with my brother, watching the blue birds on the pink curtains. Sometimes I drifted off and saw things Mum couldn't see around me. 'She's out of 'er 'ead agin,' she said arkly. 'Or else she's doin' it all on purpose. I'm gittin' fed up wi' climbin' up them stairs.'

Dad came up to see me at dinner time and hugged me, when Mum wasn't there. She never liked him to make a fuss of anyone excepting her. His newspaper was left on my bed. When Mum came back, I was trying to read it, my finger tracing each word carefully.

'I never knew you could read, Gal Audrey,' Mum snorted accusingly. 'Waa's the meanin' a' this?' She started on Father the minute he came in from work. 'What d'ye think a' that Gal Audrey?' Dad looked up fearfully, not knowing what was coming next. Mother always had something ready to upset him with.

'Why, waa's the matter with 'er now?'

'She were sittin' up in bed a-readin' your newspaper.'

'Readin' the newspaper,' Dad marvelled, ''owever did she learn ter dew that? Why, she's unly three, in't she?'

Mum gloated. The christening present he had disapproved of was justified at last.

At the end of the term, my headmistress handed Mother a little parcel. 'It's for Audrey,' she said, 'she's won the prize for the best reader.'

Mother grabbed the prize greedily. She loved something for nothing. 'I'll take that 'oom wi' me,' she said.

She was disappointed when she opened it. 'Why, it in't nothin' but a funny ole picture,' she snapped. She put it on the kitchen table. I stared at it. A little girl with silky black curls like mine, but dressed in satin and velvet. I studied my face in Mum's looking-glass. There was a difference between the girl and me. I couldn't make out what it was. It came to me then that my face was not as happy as the one on the picture, but I didn't know why.

I took it out in the garden and shyly I showed it to Clarence, the boy who lived next door. He was older than me and had a lot to say for himself. He read out the title: 'Lady Hamilton, by Gainsborough.' I was none the wiser. I showed it to Teddy, who lived further down the street.

'Is it you dressed up, Gal Audrey?' he asked. Teddy had a lopsided grin and curly hair like me.

'Yes,' I fibbed.

'You look rare smart on there,' he said, and ran off. Teddy was eight and had a bike and baggy flannels. He did a paper round and smoked with the money he got. I wrote him love letters and posted them down the drain in our alley.

Clarence was jealous. He was a gawky, lanky boy with flat slabs of greenish hair and ears that stuck out a long way. His nickname was 'Legs an' wings'. His Mum had him before she was married, but his grandparents passed him off as their own son. Everyone knew their secret, because they had a lot of rows and shouted at young Mabel about her deadly sin. They were chapel. We were church, but we didn't talk about it much, like they did.

Clarence sidled up to me when Mum was out. 'There's a ghost in your house, Gal Audrey,' he hissed. 'I know, 'cause I've seen it.'

'What's a ghost?' I asked.

'Ghosts come and get you in the middle of the night. They come up out of the graves. They're dead people.' I ran away and locked myself in the house till Mum came home.

It wasn't long before Clarence made the ghosts appear. When Mum went shopping, he got in our back window and dressed up in a sheet. He roamed about the house moaning and shrieking, then ran at me and clutched me, so that I screamed the place down.

My brother and I were afraid to go to sleep in case the ghosts got us. We had nightmares. Mum gave us an extra spoonful of syrup of figs. Then she bought us Radio Malt and Bile Beans, in case it was that.

'It's their nerves,' Grandma sniffed, her left eye twitching underneath.

'Nerves at their age,' Mother hooted, 'kids don't 'ave nerves!'

Grandma turned her lips down. 'Anyone c'n 'ave nerves, even children. Yew mark my words. Yew've got no call ter be ser 'eadstrong, Gladys.'

'I'm a-givin' you your last chance,' Mum said, as she bought the Dr De Witt's Nerve Tonic. 'If this don't work, it'll be the asylum fer both on yer. So you better git over them nerves quick, lest yew want ter be locked up in there.' We drank it down willingly this time.

Instead of the asylum we got locked in the wardrobe. Mum's big wardrobe had a big brass knob on the front. It was in two halves which came apart. But there was something wrong with it. Either it wouldn't close at all, or else it would close tight shut and not come open any more. It was a good place for playing hide and seek. Dennis and I crept in quietly and closed the door. Mum would never find us in there.

But after a while we got tired of hiding up and Mum hadn't come to find us. We hadn't been missed. When we tried to get out, the door was locked. We banged and shouted, but no one came. Frightened, we ran about inside, pulling the clothes down on top of us. Tired out with yelling and knocking, we lay down close to each other. Everything was quiet. I floated on cotton-wool clouds with a soft whirring noise in my ears. Or was it Mother talking to us? I tried to answer, but my tongue got stuck and wouldn't move.

'Thaa's funny,' Mum said in a muffled voice, 'I seen them two playin' up 'ere in the bedroom not an 'alf-hour ago, but they in't 'ere now. They must've run out down the alley. I'll 'ave ter git me coat on and look for 'em. Damn nuisance! I're got enough ter dew gittin' the dinner riddy fer 'is lordship.'

Her footsteps plodded away down the stairs. She was leaving us behind. I wanted to call out: 'Mum, here I am, come and get me.' No sound came out of my mouth and Dennis was fast asleep, snoring out loud in my ears. I clutched at his face with my hands, but he wouldn't wake up.

All at once, Mum was holding a cup of milk to my lips and I was lying stretched out on the couch in our living-room. Our neighbour, young Mabel, was staring down at me and cradling Dennis in her arms. Mum was crying. I didn't know why.

"Owever did they git inter that damn wardrobe? Worry my life out, they do. It's deliberate badness. I'll take a stick to them once they're better.'

I suppose we weren't meant to die that day. Mother had put a stop to it. But death was in the air and Father was the next victim.

It was Sunday morning, the day when Dad collected his *News of the World* from Granny's house. He'd been in the habit of having it delivered to his mother's cottage when he was single and no one had ever changed the order, though he'd been married for years. It was proof of his disloyalty to Mum. She claimed he went there to talk about her behind her back, to his mother. That was why he always came home in a bad mood of a Sunday, after she'd slaved all morning to get the dinner ready.

'Call yerself a man?' Mum bawled. 'Leavin' yer wife and two kids on a Sunday mornin', with the dinner ter cook and all the 'ousework ter do! Poshin' y'rself up ter go an' see y'r ole woman. They all know what she's like when she 'as a drop. Talk a' the city, she is.' Mum battered the coconut matting with her short-brush, down on her knees with a red face, her curlers rattling.

'Shut yew up,' Dad said, 'we know she's no angel. She're 'ad a 'ard life, in't she?'

He glared at himself in the looking-glass and stropped his razor up and down on the leather strap that hung from the back of the door. His enamel mug was full of soap with the brush stuck in the middle.

"Sides, what make yew think I want ter go down there in the pourin' rain? Yew got ter slog y'r guts out all the week, then when yew wants ter take a stroll, it's got ter rain.'

'There's no pleasin' yew,' Mum snarled. 'Allus grumblin'! Yew want ter think y'rself lucky y'r got y'r 'ealth an' strength. You c'd be blind an' deaf an' dumb, like some pore people.'

'Think meself lucky 'cause I'm poor an' don't know where the next ha'penny's comin' from! Yew make me smile.' He went on shaving himself carefully, holding his nose up in the air with two fingers while he did his top lip, scraping away with his old cut-throat razor, collecting the lather as it foamed over the blade. One minute he was peering into the glass, the next he staggered back with blood pumping out of his Adam's apple, pouring over his tucked-in collar and shirt front. Mother had wrenched the mat from under his feet and the blade had slit his throat.

'Whatever 'ave yew done?' Mum scrambled up, realising she had gone too far. White and horrified, Father pulled the edges of the wound together with his fingers. He said nothing. Mum got a towel and tied it tight round his neck. He ran straight out of the house as he was and didn't stop till he got to the hospital. The tourniquet must have saved his life. He got there without losing all his blood. But he had twenty-seven stitches in his throat.

'Whatever made you do such a thing, man!' the doctor barked at Dad. 'I sh'll have to report this, you know. It's against the law to cut your throat.'

'Why sir, it were a pure accident,' Father blurted out. 'The wife were doin' 'er 'ousework as usual an' she 'appened to jerk the mat from under me feet. She never noticed I were a-standin' on it at the time.'

'Accident, you say. Well man, we'll overlook it this time. But don't try it again.'

'I sh'll never know 'owever I got to that 'ospital in time,' Father gasped when he got home. He was swathed in lint and bandages that forced his head back, so that he looked down his long nose at us. He lay on the couch for the rest of the day and Mother had to wait on him.

Next morning, he got up as usual and went off to work. But that was the last of his Sunday morning outings. The *News of the World* came to *our* house after that.

Mum looked down on Dad; but no one else did. He was looked up to at work. Whenever a machine went wrong, they called for Charlie Emms. He was an electrician and could wire up the whole factory, if he wanted to. We were one of the first families in the street to have an electric kettle that plugged into a hole in the wall. Dad worked long hours if there was a breakdown at the firm and he got tired out. That was how he got his arm trapped in a machine.

'A rare ole state 'e were in,' Mother crowed, 'gashed right open from top ter bottom that arm were. Yew c'd reg'lar see the buu'n, clean as a whistle.' Mum's eyes sparkled. She enjoyed talking about it.

Mr Egerton, Father's chargehand, came to visit him while he was on the club. Mother liked Mr Egerton. He stood on the doorstep, burly in his raincoat, looking as though he knew a thing or two. When he lifted his hat to Mum, I noticed he had a pointed head. I liked heads that were round and a bit flat on top, like Dad's. Swanky as he looked in his Burton's made-to-measure, Mr Egerton had sharp eyes and teeth to match.

'You'll be 'is little missus then,' he said, all smarmy, to Mother. 'Fer one minute I thought you might a' bin 'is daughter.'

Mum's face changed for the better. 'There in't no need ter stand out there in the cold, Mr Egerton. Dew yew come in an' I'll put the kittle on.'

Father was in his shirt-sleeves, one arm in a sling. He tore upstairs for his jacket, before shaking hands awkwardly with his left.

Mr Egerton made a performance of wiping his boots. 'And how are you, man?' he boomed in a bossy voice. 'Quite fit fer work again now, are yer?'

'I in't ser bad, master,' Dad hedged, with a long face. 'It's just the shock wot it's left me with. The stitches 'ave bin took out, but I got a cer-stifficate till Friday.'

'Capital!' Mr Egerton roared, banging Father on the back. 'Then we sh'll see yew back on the floor come Saturday morning fer sure, keen as mustard. 'Zat right, man?'

Dad mooched round the room, his empty sleeve flapping and his Adam's apple sticking out because he hadn't got his collar on yet. 'Reckon so, master,' he agreed dismally.

'I come up from the works with 'is money,' Mr Egerton confided.

Mum's hand shot out. 'I'll take care a' that then,' she snapped, ''e'll unly squander it.' But he didn't hand it over and Mum went over to the glass and ran a comb through her hair.

''E'll be that pleased to make a start again,' she laughed gaily. She was having a hard job getting the comb through her mop. It was a bit matted in places. 'It's ever so thick, my wool. We're all got plenty a' 'air in my fam'ly.' She smiled and started humming: 'All By Y'rself in the Moonlight'.

'There ain't no sense,
Sittin' on a fence,
All by y'rself in the moonlight.'

'Bin gittin' under yer feet, 'as 'e?' Mr Egerton winked at her.

'My stars, I sh'd think 'e 'ave. 'E's bin givin' me the 'ump. 'E will keep on makin' up that fire. I mean ter say, 'e know the price a' coal.'

She managed to keep her voice under control, so Mr Egerton wouldn't go and say she was a nagger. But Dad was cut to the quick in front of his boss. 'My heart alive,' he snorted, his eyes wild, 'I take on my oath I in't touched that fire. Thaa's more 'n I dare dew.'

'Now, now, Charlie, temper, temper,' Mr Egerton shook a stubby finger at Dad, like a child.

'Yer a stinkin' liar!' Mother snarled, forgetting herself, 'I seen yer wi' me own eyes.' Mum and Dad faced each other like two mad dogs.

Mr Egerton put his oar in. 'But yew 'ave bin allowed extra fer y'r coal, 'aven't yew, man? Why, we collected for yew last week, on the shop floor. I chipped in meself, as I recall.' He bit hard into one of Mum's short cakes. It was a bit dry and crumbs showered off his front teeth. He laid it down on the table-cloth.

'I b'lieve we did get an extra 'undred,' Father admitted.

'An extra 'undred!' Mum shrieked. 'I in't seen no extra 'undreds 'ere! There in't bin nothin' left in that coal'ouse, yew c'n see fer y'self.' She started for the door to prove it.

Mr Egerton slurped his tea importantly, frowned, took out a big handkerchief, wiped his moustache and blew his nose. We waited to hear what he would say next. 'Are yew quite certain a' that, Mrs Emms?' he asked solemnly. 'If you are, I sh'll 'ave ter see inter this.'

'I wu'nt put it past 'em ter dew me out on it,' Mum whimpered, 'it wu'nt be the fuu'st time. 'E never stick up fer 'is rights, an' they shit on 'im down-a that firm, left, right and centre.'

'Stuu'n me blue,' Father muttered, 'we're orf. It alwus 'as ter be me, don't it?' As if in sympathy, the last few cinders rattled down into the hearth and fizzled out.

'Gal Audrey!' Mum rounded on me. 'I told yew ter give that fire a good poke. Din't yew 'ear me?' I jumped up from the table where I was doing my homework and threw the rest of the coal on quickly. No one took any notice, so I sat down again.

'Now, Mrs Emms, don't take on. Charlie's in the Oddfellows,

in't 'e?' He turned towards Mother, realising she was the one in charge.

'A paltry penny a week,' Mum said bitterly, 'that's all 'e's in for. That don't go far, when yer got them 'ot fermintations ter pay for.'

The kettle went on boiling and the kitchen was full of steam. 'Make us another pot, Gal Audrey.' I poured out a cup. She took one sip and spat it out all over the table. 'Thaa's tack, that is. Audrey's water, is wot we calls it. I like a good cup meself.' I threw in another spoonful and stirred the pot hard. Mum was getting peevish. When she poured herself another cup, the leaves came floating to the top. She heaved a sigh in Mr Egerton's direction and shook her head sadly. 'Yew can't put ole 'eads on young shoulders, can yew?'

'Nice drop a' wallpaper yew got in 'ere, very 'omely.' Mr Egerton changed the subject, as he took a second cup through a tea-strainer.

'I 'ung that meself. 'E can't dew paperin',' Mum chimed in eagerly. ''E can't dew nuthin'. I 'as ter dew the lot, an' I gits no appreciation, neether,' she bleated.

'Well, never you mind, Mrs Emms, there's others wot appreciate it, y'know.' His glance was so full of pity that Mother's lip quivered. She realised how hard done by she was. Then he glanced sideways at Dad. 'All right then, Charlie,' he bawled, 'I'd better be a-gettin' back ter the bench. It's all very well fer gentlemen of leisure. I'll tell 'em down the firm, yer fit as a fiddle now.'

Father didn't answer. He pocketed the money lying on the table as the door slammed behind Mr Egerton. 'Yew din't 'alf kowtow ter 'im,' he scowled, pinging his braces with his one good thumb.

''E's wot I calls a *man*!' she spat out. She went straight upstairs and came down a few minutes later with her black court shoes on. It was a funny time of the day to change into her best shoes, but you never knew what Mum was going to do next.

Mr Egerton was as good as his word. He looked into it. A few days later, there was a knock at the door and the two Misses Jeremiah Colman stood there. They wore poke bonnets and high collars pinned up with silver Mizpah brooches. It was their only frippery. Mum was highly honoured seeing the owners of Dad's firm on her doorstep.

'Oh, dew yew come in,' she beamed. They studied the doormat carefully to see if it was dirty before they walked on it. 'Thaa's a nice day, in't it?' Mum ignored the pouring rain. There was no answer. They looked down their long noses at her. They both had long ginger hairs on their upper lips and their mouths pointed downwards at the corners. They smelt of carbolic, like the drains.

'Will yer 'ave a cup a' tea?' Mum twittered, pulling two chairs out. One Miss Colman had a limp and sat down heavily. Their hobble skirts crackled and they exchanged warning glances.

'Tea? Certainly not, Mrs Emms, we don't drink stimulants,' they snapped.

'Whatever's that?' Mum quacked, looking worried.

'Why, Mrs Emms, tea, coffee, cocoa, they're stimulants, didn't you know?'

'Well, I never did,' Mum clicked her tongue. 'Coffee, we never did 'ave, nor like tew 'ave in this 'ouse. I 'ad an auntie wot killed 'erself wi' coffee. Camp coffee it were. Allus 'ave it, she would. Course, in the end 'er kidneys got blocked up and she went bright yaller all over. Blew up like a balloon an' died. They cuun't squash 'er inter 'er corfin when it come tew it. Coffee's a poison, an' thaa's a fack. So wot'll yew 'ave then? I're got a bottle a' that there barley water wot's 'anded out by the firm. No one'll touch it 'ere, 'cause it's sich a funny colour.' Mum blushed, remembering whom she was talking to. 'Course, you'd know all about that, wun't yew?'

One sister started tittering, hand to her mouth. The other stopped her with a look that was more like a blow. They glared down at their high-buttoned boots sticking out under black skirts. So did I. They had legs like matchsticks and the biggest feet I had ever seen on the end of them.

'Now, Mrs Emms,' said the one who did all the talking, 'we have been asked to visit you. We were notified you were without any coal. Yet we notice you've got a good fire burning in your hearth. So why is that, Mrs Emms?'

I stared at Mum. How would she get out of that? But her brain worked fast. 'Why, thaa's a shovelful wot I lent orf a' me sister this mornin'. We wus so shiverin' a-cold in this 'ouse,' she explained, her blue eyes wide and truthful. 'We're bin perishin' this last few weeks, ever since me 'usban' got 'is arm crushed in that machine down-a the warks. 'E's bin on the club, yer see. Ripped 'is arm ter pieces. All the flesh was 'angin' orf of it, an' the buu'ns sticking out. Blood everywhere there was. They was goin' ter cut it right orf, but 'e wouldn't let 'em. 'E said as 'ow 'e might need that arm. 'E's very 'eadstrong, my 'usban'. Thinks 'e know better than doctors, 'e does.'

'We know all about the case, Mrs Emms. There's no need to tell us the details. We just want the facts. We only give to deserving cases and we have to make sure you deserve our help first.'

They sipped the barley water out of two odd cups. We hadn't got any glasses.

'Do you read the Bible, little girl?'

'Read? Why she'll read the eyes out a' 'er 'ead, if I let 'er,' Mum answered for me. 'She know portree, an' all.'

Both sisters' lips parted slowly and they leered at me. It was hard for their faces to give a proper smile. 'And which poet do you read, little girl?'

Terrified of their hairy faces and big feet, I lost my voice. 'I like Shelley,' I whispered.

'Yis, thaa's right, I caught 'er reading Sherry in bed the other night. Not that I 'old wi' readin' in bed.'

'Not Sherry, Mum,' I said, 'Shelley.'

'Don't yew contradick me, Gal Audrey, front a' company,' she snorted, getting nasty. The Misses Colman got up quickly, leaving their barley water. They glared at Mum's lisle stockings, concertina-ed round her stocky legs, and her cable-stitch cardigan with the holes under the arms where she sweated.

'Now, Mrs Emms, say no more. We must be off. We have to be present at a charity meeting at the Stuart Hall. We may see our way to allowing you five shillings towards your coal.' They marched to the door.

Mum barred the way. 'An' when will I be a-gettin' it?' she asked in a loud voice.

They took up their black umbrellas and flapped them twice, showering the coconut matting. 'That depends on a lot of things, Mrs Emms,' one said peevishly. 'The firm is on short-time, as you know. Our sinking fund is low. Our calls are many. There are good people starving all over the world. You're one of the lucky ones, Mrs Emms. Go sparing, rein yourself in. We lead a very Spartan existence ourselves, you know.'

Mum slammed the door hard. 'What do that mean?' she demanded.

'It means not eating much, Mum.'

'Cheek on it!' Mum roared. 'Them as got a 'alf-dozen flunkeys at their beck an' call, an' thousands in the bank, tellin' me ter starve meself! Two ole scarecrows, like them. Wot do they want ter go round dressed up like that for? Them ole bonnets went out wi' the ark.'

She hunched up her shoulders and dragged her hair back from her face, making her eyes cross. 'I cuu'nt look like them, if I tried.' She burst out laughing. 'Shove some coal on that fire, Gal Audrey. They made the whool 'ouse go cold. Couple a' wizened-up ole maids! All froozen up. Y'r Father'd soon warm them up, once 'e'd got a drop a' stout in 'im. Thaa's wot they could do with. That'd put a stop ter their gallivantin' round doin' good works in that ole clobber. I din't like them openin' umber'ellas in this 'ouse, neether. Thaa's a sure sign a' sickness. Good job they din't ask ter see round the place,' she chuckled. 'I in't even emptied my chamber yit. If it 'ad 've bin my mother wot they snubbed, she'd a' poured the whool lot over 'em out a' the bedroom winder, bonnets an' all.'

She threw the barley water down the sink and made a cup of tea. 'Let's 'ave a couple a' rounds a' toost.' I held out the toasting fork in front of the flames. Mum pulled up her chair and spread the butter thick.

'Yew know 'ow they gits like that, don't yer?' she gulped between mouthfuls. 'All of a twitch? It's 'cause they in't never 'ad no enjoyment. They don't never know wot it's like tew 'ave a drop a' stout on a Saturday night an' a nice lay-in wi' y'r 'usban' on a Sunday mornin'. 'Cause they in't never 'ad no 'usban's. They go rushin' orf ter chuu'ch instead. They can't bear the sight a' theirselves in the glass, 'cause no one else can eether. Dried up ole bags a' buu'ns, both on 'em. 'Oo want them? They don't even want theirselves. Wi' all their thousands they don't know the meanin' er pleasure. A nice plate a' cockles, or 'ot peas down a' the market. They don't go nowhere 'cause they're scared stiff a' men. Thaa's why they've growed them 'airs all over their clocks. It's ter warn the men ter keep orf, yer see.

'Now, I'll tell yer suffin' about them, unly don't yew let it go any further. One of 'em 'ad a sweet'eart years ago, a-down a' the warks. Unly an ord'nary boy, 'e were, in the flour mill. But 'e were nice-lookin' an' twenty-one. She were sixteen an' a bit of a frump. Still, 'e liked 'er. They was found tergether be'ind the flour bags, a-sloppin' an a-kissin'. 'E swore blind 'e wanted ter marry 'er. Course, they give 'im the sack an' orfered 'im another job wi' better money, up in 'Ull. 'E ask 'er ter go with 'im an' she tried to do a bunk. But she got packed orf ter Switz-lan' ter learn 'ow ter talk Swiss.'

'You mean French, Mum.'

'That's it. Yer the ed-jicated one, not me.'

'Course, she never did git married,' Mum nodded her head gravely and buttered the last round of toast. 'She come back 'oom on crutches. Brook 'cr lcg in seven places she did, a-slidin' down them mountains on a bit a' wood wot they 'ave. She never could get about prop'ly after that. Allus 'ad a limp.'

I lifted my legs and stared at my white ankle-socks. 'That must a' bin rotten, Mum.'

'Thaa's when she got connected with the chuu'ch an' started doin' good warks. She come in 'andy ter the vicar, 'cause a lot on 'em down the firm joined as well, ter git on the right side of 'er father, ole Sir Jeremiah.

'There were that Mr Swift, fer one. 'E got a foreman's job through bein' a sidesman. 'E wus unly an ordinary tradesman like y'r Dad. But 'e's got on. True Christian, 'e is, Mr Swift. Very morose with it. 'Im an' 'is missus never 'ad a stick a' furnit-cher in their 'ouse till 'e got saved. Yew know 'oo I mean, live down the end 'ere.'

I nodded. I knew which one was Mr Swift. I had to keep out of his way, or he might put his hands up my dress when I was playing on the swings. But Mum never knew about that.

'Them sort a' Christians,' Mum mused, 'they 'aven't never found out which way their arse 'ang, an' thaa's a fack.'

5
A Plaster Saint

Mum dressed me up like a doll, though she could ill afford it. It was her way of making up for the way she treated me. But it made me stand out from other children and it meant I had to keep clean. As soon as I got home from school I put on my pinafore before I went out to play. I was small for my age, with a chubby face, tangled black curls and big puzzled eyes. So much was a mystery to me that I was always trying to find out things.

One place I found mysterious was the churchyard with the graves of dead people. It was at the bottom of St Julian's Street where I lived.

'Come on, Katie,' I called, 'let's go and play at St Julian's.' The old flint wall was spiked with glass at the top, but rain had worn it smooth. We could easily climb over.

'I'm comin' as well, Gal Audrey.' My brother swung his legs over. He was bigger and stronger than I was. 'Look out fer the sexton though.'

We played hide and seek among the graves, hiding behind the tall cypresses and picking the cowslips and cuckoo pints; chasing the butterflies.

In the middle of the churchyard stood a black marble tomb covered with writing. But you couldn't read it. If you ran round it three times and knocked hard, you could hear the dead body inside groan.

'Quick, Katie,' I squealed and skipped behind the tomb. The grass was so tall it closed over my head and Katie ran past giggling. I pressed myself hard against the stone. It was freezing. I waited for my brother Dennis to come and find me. Then I heard a bloodcurdling yell: 'Wooh! Ooh, ooh!'

I screamed and bolted before the dead body could come out. I ran straight into the church and the door slammed behind me with a grinding noise. It was dim and scary. Two candles burnt on the altar. I hid in the choir stalls, my heart thumping.

It was quiet and peaceful in the flickering light and after a while I plucked up courage. I was curious to have a good look round as there was no one about. There was a smell of incense and tallow from the candles. I tiptoed from statue to monument, fingering the silver altar-cloth. A big leather Bible with a gold lock on it lay open. I peeped in, then shrank back. The words were from Ezekiel: 'I will open your graves and cause you to come up.' It must be meant for me. Someone knew I was there. I swivelled round and blundered straight into a black figure gliding along the aisle. I fell down with a shriek.

'Whatever is the matter, little girl?' said a gentle voice. I opened my eyes. It wasn't a dead person, but a nun. She helped me up. Her eyes were calm and grey, like Dad's, with sloping eyebrows.

'I'm ever so sorry,' I panted. 'I was just going home.'

'You *are* in a hurry, can't you stop a minute?' I expected her to be angry, but she was smiling. 'Now dear, tell me who you are and I'll tell you who I am.'

'I'm Audrey Emms,' I whispered, finding my tongue. 'I live in St Julian's Street.'

She bent down and studied my face. 'I remember you,' she said, 'you were the doll in the box, who danced for us at the social.' Her voice was clear and musical. She didn't talk Norfolk like us.

'Yes, that's right,' I said. We both laughed. It was strange to be treated like someone who really mattered and not just a child.

'Well Audrey, I'm Sister Dorothea and I work for this church and the Lady Julian.' Her white wimple seemed to spring right out of her high forehead, as though it were part of her face. I had seen a painting just like her on the church wall. I pointed to it. 'Is that a picture of you, Sister?' I asked shyly.

'Oh no,' she chuckled, 'not me. That's Lady Julian. You've heard of her, haven't you?' I shook my head and stared at the painting again; the sad face with a golden halo. Down at her feet crouched a small cat with frightened eyes.

'Well, Audrey, this church is named after her. She used to have an open window for the poor, where the starving came to get food.'

'Where did she get it from?' I asked.

'Ah, that is one of God's mysteries. She asked Him to provide and He did. She was a great saint. She saw Our Lord in a dream, you know.' Sister Dorothea's eyes were misty, she seemed far away, then she remembered me again. 'Now Audrey, run along, your mother will be worried.'

My brother was on the swing when I ran in the back gate. I pushed him off. 'You've had your turn,' I said.

'Where'd yew git to?' he shouted.

'I went in the church and I met Saint Julian,' I said proudly. I let my head fall back, as I worked myself up on the swing. It was just like being a bird and flying up to the tops of the trees.

'You liar,' he shrilled, 'you're always tellin' lies, in't yew?'

I ignored him. He wouldn't understand. 'Where's Mum?' I asked.

'She's out.'

I went indoors and set the table for tea. Mum burst in, flinging the door wide open, so it banged against the couch. You could tell it was her, without even looking. Dad always let himself in very quietly. She flung her basket down and kicked off her shoes. 'My blummin' feet ache,' she moaned, 'git the kittle on, Gal Audrey.'

When Dad came in, she barked: 'I never 'eard yew come through that door. Yew creep about this 'ouse like a blummin' rat.' She didn't say 'mouse', that was too good for him.

'Well, yew knew I was 'ere. No need ter make sich a song an' dance about it.'

'I likes tew 'ear when people come inter this 'ouse. I 'ate them 'oo creep about.'

''Oo's creepin' about? I unly walk, same's everyone else.'

'My heart alive,' she bellowed, 'yew don't 'alf make me raw. Allus contradictin'.' She stuffed grapes into her mouth and began spitting pips all over the room. Her hands moved back and forth to her lips monotonously, while her eyes were fixed on the *Evening News*. I wanted to tell her about Sister Dorothea, but I kept it to myself. Then she stopped munching and read out the headlines. '*Seveered head found in woman's dustbin*. Now waddya' think a' that? I dunno what this city's a-cummin' to. What do that mean – *seveered*?'

'You mean severed 'ead,' Dad corrected her slowly, 'why, it mean cut off.'

'No need ter be sarky,' Mum snapped, ignoring his explanation. 'Did yew git me any sweets this week?'

'I wondered when yew was goin' ter ask,' Dad sounded relieved.

'I're allus got ter ask yew fuu'st, 'aven't I? You'd never orfer, would yer!'

Friday nights Dad always brought home a quarter of toffees. There would be a row if he forgot. He felt in the pocket of his old raincoat. 'Jus' slipped me mind, 'ere y'are.'

Mum grabbed the bag and glared inside. 'Cuu'nt yew git me Blue Bird? These in't wot I like.'

Dad scratched his head in despair. 'I could a' sworn yew ask fer Sharps.'

'Sharps! That I never. Yew c'n stick Sharps. Yer the unly one 'ere wot likes Sharps. Thaa's why yew bought 'em, I s'puz.'

'I don't trouble whether I 'ave a sweet from one year's end ter the next. Sweets don't worry me,' Dad protested. But it didn't do him any good.

'So yew reckin,' she snarled, 'but I know different. Yer a guts when it come ter suffin' yew like, same as everyone else.'

I realised she was getting herself wound up when she started on the cat. 'My law, that blasted Minnie don't 'alf hum. I reckin she're got fleas agin.' She caught Minnie by the tail and started hunting through her soft ginger fur. The more she struggled, the more Mum tightened her grip. She would pull her to bits. I couldn't bear the sight. I picked up my *Pip, Squeak and Wilfred* annual and went to bed.

I dreamt Sister Dorothea came into my bedroom and started undressing herself. I was worried in case there was nothing underneath her black clothes, she might not have a proper body. She wasn't a bit like Mum, who was all body, especially when she took off her stays. Layers of clothes came off Sister Dorothea, like the surprise parcel you passed round at Christmas. She rustled like paper as well. Maybe it was her bones. I closed my eyes in the dream as she got to her vest. When I opened them, she had changed into a fairy with a magic wand and we were standing in the church, with all the candles glowing. Then I heard Mum shrieking at me. 'Come yew on, Gal Audrey. Git up an' run an errand fer me.' The sunshine streamed in my window and I forgot all about Sister Dorothea.

When I got home from school that day, the lace table-cloth was on the table, with a plate of thin bread and butter. Mum was excited. 'What d'ye think, Gal Audrey? Sister Dorothea's bin 'ere.'

'Whatever for?'

'She want yew ter join 'er Bible Class. Yer 'ighly honoured, my lady. She only pick out them with a vacation.'

'What's a vacation, Mum?' Somehow I thought it meant a seaside holiday. I sipped my milk. Mum had just found out that children were meant to have it instead of tea.

Mum pondered on the word. 'It mean yew could be a nun like 'er, if yew set y'r 'eart on it. Yew'd 'ave ter make y'r mind up pretty quick, a' course. They 'as to put yer name down fer it well in advance.'

'A nun,' I echoed. Then a thought struck me. 'But I'd have to have all my hair cut off,' I wailed, almost crying.

Mum gave me a shifty glance. She set store by my hair. So did the neighbours, who said it was pretty and a credit to Mum, even though it was dark and not fair, like her people.

'Well, it's up ter yew what yew dew. I'm not pushin' yew inter nuthin'. 'Sides, I can't stand 'ere mardlin', 'e'll be in fer 'is grub direckly.'

While I set the table, Mum went on talking. 'She's a real lady, that Sister. Put me in mind er me Grandmother. It's too far back fer yew ter remember. 'Er name were Polly. She were a real lady, an' all. My ole Grandfa wun't nuthin' good enough fer 'er. Allus shoutin' an' bawlin', that was 'im. She were quiet an' nicely spoken. She got fed up wi' 'im an' 'is swearin'. In the end she say: "I'll put a stop tew 'im." She went outside ter the closet. She put a glove on 'er 'and and she scooped up a 'andful a' shit. Soon's 'e started blasphemin', she rammed it right inter 'is gob.' Mum yelped with laughter, her sides shaking. 'Me Grandfa never used language no more in front of 'er. She finished 'is swearin' fer good.'

After tea, Mum put her hair in papers and went back to the subject of Sister Dorothea. 'Course, they're marvellous, them sisters. My ole Grandma 'ad them in ter lay 'er out. They washed 'er, dressed 'er up lovely, put 'er teeth in. She looked a treat. They emptied 'er slops an' all. Wun't take nuthin' fer it, neether. Did it all fer the Lord.'

It was the first time I'd heard Mum praise up anyone. She wanted me to go to that Bible Class, that must be it. So I said I would.

Mum wrapped up one of her coconut macaroons for Sister. 'She'll enjoy this with 'er tea,' she said. I carried it carefully. Sister Dorothea's eyes twinkled. 'Thank your Mum for me, Audrey, but I'm afraid I can't eat it myself. It's Lent. We'll take it to old Mrs Pashley, she's in bed with dropsy.' I decided I wouldn't tell Mum.

The Bible Class was five old ladies in big hats fastened on to their heads with beaded pins like little truncheons. Their feet stuck out under long skirts and they looked as though they could smell something gone bad. Old Mother Rudd was there. Mum said she put curses on people. You had to keep out of her way, in case she fixed her evil eye on you.

Sister Dorothea read to us in her gentle voice, now and again smiling at me. I watched her long pale face and her hands, fluttering like birds caught in her black robes. I didn't listen to what she said, but a feeling of contentment came over me. On the way home she held my hand and said: 'Your Mother told me you wrote poetry, Audrey.'

I blushed. Fancy Mum telling Sister Dorothea about that! I had to admit it now. 'You must let me read some. I'm very fond of poetry.'

The idea of showing her my poems made me feel shivery. Mum thought I was peculiar, writing poetry. Then my brother had chanted: 'Okey, pokey, penny a lump, the more yew eat the more yew trump,' and Mum had flown at him and clipped his lug.

But now it was being taken seriously. When I got home, I copied out

The Fireside

On rainy days
When I feel sad,
I watch the blaze –
It makes me glad.

Mum pokes the coal,
And I can see,
Mountains roll
Quite silently!

And faces come,
Smile, and go,
I'm here with Mum
In the fire's glow.

I put it in an envelope and left it in the church. Sister Dorothea kept it. She wrote me a letter:

Dear Audrey,
Thank you for your lovely poem. You are really clever to write it. Your words make me see things in a different way.
Your sincere friend,
Sister Dorothea.

I put it under my pillow and read it over again. I thought about her. How different she was from Mum; but a bit like me. I was not just Mum's Gal Audrey. I was myself, after all. Dad said everyone had to be themselves. They couldn't be other people. Now I knew what he meant. I was different. I had a lot of thoughts that belonged to me and no one else. All my secrets they were. Perhaps I would tell Sister Dorothea about my secrets. She would understand. I felt happy, looking forward to it.

But Mum put a stop to it. She glared at me when I put a picture of Mary and Jesus on my dressing-table. 'I don't 'old with all this worshippin' a' graven images an' plaster saints, like they does at St Julian's. God never meant people tew act like that.'

The next Sunday Mum sent me to Lady Lane Chapel instead. They were all Methodists there and hadn't got any nuns, or saints. 'But Mum,' I said, 'you reckoned the Little Sisters were marvellous.'

'I're changed me mind,' was all she would say.

6
A Different World

'She come to my door when I were in me labour, a-stirrin' up strife, the ole bitch. Soon's ever she knocked, all me pains stopped. I never 'ad another one till she buzzed orf agin. Put the 'fluence on me, she did.' Mother nodded her head three times as she dug down into the sugar bowl. She was going on about Father's mother again. She couldn't forget the past and Granny's treachery.

' "I're brought yer a nice custard, Gladys," she say ter me, all smarmy. "I thought you'd 'ave that wi' yer tea." Course, I threw that straight down the sink once she'd slung 'er 'ook. No tellin' wot she might a' put in that.' She stirred her cup viciously. 'She 'ad 'er best 'at on, an' all. "I thought that child 'ad a' bin borned be now. Yer overdue, in't yer?" 'Ow did she know that? Nosy ole beggar!

' "Overdue!" I say. "'Ow d'ye know I'm overdue? It'll come when it's a mind to, an' don't let anyone tell yew any different". I slammed the door in 'er face. Like a diddicoy, she were, 'is mother. Funny shape an' all, in that 'opsack costume, what she 'ad on. Got 'erself up, she 'ad. "Sling your 'ook," I say to 'er.

'It were the wuss't thing I could a' done. She got 'er own back on me. Three days I wus in me labour. Three days!' Mother bleated. 'They 'ad ter give me the twilight sleep, an' all. Dr Murphy turned me over fer dead. 'E shruck out, "She's gorn, Mrs Bland," (that were the midwife). Course, they 'ad ter use instewments in the end, ter git 'im 'ere.'

She pointed at my brother, who was eating his dinner with a gloomy face. He shifted his feet, then clumped out, down the garden.

'She put a cuss on me,' Mum snarled. 'But that weren't the reason why she come that day. She reckined she'd take yew orf a' me 'ands fer the day. But I were one too many fer 'er. "Certainly not", I say tew 'er. "Yew've got y'r best 'at on, so I reckon yer bound fer the pub and I'm not 'avin' my little mawther go in no pubs." So I kept yew wi' me.'

I smiled up at Mum, not sure whether to thank her. But she didn't expect me to say anything, she just droned on while she moved the ornaments on the mantelpiece to get at the dust.

'The doctor had to clamp the irons round a' y'r brother's 'ead an' heave hard.' Mum puffed as she said it. 'Mrs Bland pulled in the other direction. Course I cuun't walk fer weeks after. I never wanted ter come round no more, after that lot. But they forced me to. I spewed up the claraform an' Mrs Bland made me a cup a' beef tea. "Stop that groanin'," she say, "we're 'avin' enough trouble, as it is. Look 'ow yer made me sweat, Mrs Emms!"

'Next thing I knew I'd gorn onconscious agin. So they sent fer me Mother. Y'r Dad was at work, but they never called 'im out. Course, it upset me Mother, on account of she hadn't set foot outside fer years with 'er 'eart. But when they said I was goin' she put 'er 'at an' coat on and she come, wi' my sister Eunie in tow. If I'd a' known she'd bring 'er, I would a-locked up all me cupboards first.

'I were on me last gasp when me Mother come up them stairs. First thing she say ter me were: "Gal Gladdy, yew better git up out a' that bed, 'cause Eunie's in your pantry a-pinchin' your butter." ' Mum glared at me, red and angry as she remembered it all.

'Jest yew picture that, Gal Audrey,' she fumed, 'thaa's the sort a' sister I 'ad, pinchin' me butter when I were on me death-bed! An' that were when 'e were born, black an' blue from them instewments an' screamin' 'is 'ead orf.'

Mum finished the dusting, spat on the duster and cleaned the looking-glass. I went outside to find my brother. He was a big strong boy now, but that winter he got the croup.

'Stop that damn corfin'!' Mum shouted in the middle of the night. But he wouldn't stop. Mum took us to Dr Murphy.

'I'm afraid, Mrs Emms, it's tonsils and adenoids to come out. We'd better get Audrey's out as well, just in case. Now, I'll make an appointment for them to go in.'

Mum opened the letter a few days later. 'Norfic an' Norwich 'Orspital, nine a'clock termorrer mornin',' she told Dad.

'I'll be at work then,' Dad said.

Mother left us in the hospital crying, but she was back within the hour. She couldn't keep away. We were her flesh and blood. 'I 'ad a pree'monition,' she told us afterwards. She was right. My brother developed blood poisoning and nearly died. But Mum wouldn't let him go. She sat by the bed day and night, swearing at the doctors, saying she would report them if anything happened to her boy. 'I walked round and round that 'orspital. I could 'ear that Boy Dennis a-cryin' in there. I knew I shuu'nt a' left 'im.' But Dennis was saved.

It wasn't long before Mother pushed the two of us home in the big black pram. All my brother said was: 'Take me 'oom ter see my Daddy.' He was still poorly and his voice had gone very deep. She laid us on the rexine couch in the living-room and gave us Parrish's Food, out of a brown bottle. It tasted of blood. My throat was still raw and bleeding.

The operation was supposed to cure my catarrh and Dennis's cough. But it didn't. I was still delicate and he continued to have the croup.

'It's this 'ouse,' Mum fretted. The minute Dad's face appeared in the doorway, she bawled at him, 'I'm movin' out a' this 'ouse. I've made me mind up. There in't nuthin' yew can do about it.'

'Move?' Father was shocked. 'Whatcver dew yew mean? I'm not movin'. My ole man an' woman 'ave lived in the same 'ouse all their lives an' I'm goin' ter dew the same.'

'I'm not lettin' these children live in the wet. 'Ave yew seen them walls?'

'Walls, wot walls?' Father was scared. 'Waa's wrong wi' the walls?'

'Water a-runnin' down 'em,' she fumed, 'oughter be condemned. I'm gittin' a council 'ouse.'

'Barmy, thaa's wot y'are,' Father blew up for once. 'We can't afford no council 'ouses. Seven-an'-six a week I pay fer this an' thaa's more 'n I c'n afford alriddy. 'Sides, I're got ter be near the warks, 'aven't I?'

It was a long speech for Father. We lived in a tall narrow house Father rented from Uncle John Minns, who made tombstones for the cemetery. Mother had an underground kitchen with hardly any light, except from the brick copper that glowed when she set fire to the sticks and boiled her washing.

Mother stormed up the City Hall. 'I'm entitled tew a council 'ouse. I're got a doctor's cer-stifficate ter prove it.'

'Well, Mrs Emms, we can put your name down,' the council man coughed nervously, 'but I don't hold out too much hopes.'

A few days later, she went back again, leaned on the counter and banged the bell incessantly. 'I'm goin' tew 'ave another one, an' I got two alriddy,' she said, piping her eye.

'Now, Mrs Emms, I've promised to do everything I can for you,' the man soothed.

'It's not enough,' she bawled. 'Sich as yew don't know nuthin' about sich as us. I s'puz yew got a nice 'ouse y'rself out a' the council. Yer lookin' after number one and letting the rest of us go an' shit!'

'Please Mrs Emms, don't use language here. I'm doing my best.' It wasn't long before we were allocated a house. Mum looked it over and banged on the bell at the City Hall again.

'That 'ouse what you palmed me orf with in't no good. I don't want it. There in't no shops close to. There in't no school fer me kids ter go tew neether.' The corporation was building on the outskirts of Norwich, in the middle of a swampy area called Mousehold.

Mother waved her arms in the air, shouting and creating a stir in front of the queue. So we got a nice six-roomed house not far from the shops and, in spite of Dad's forebodings, we moved.

While Mum was carrying her chiffonier off the wheelbarrow, I ran down to the end of the road and found we were overlooking a railway cutting where the goods trains shunted past. I climbed over the railings and stared round. On the far side of the tracks it was all sunshine. Banks of daisies and clover stretched for miles. There were trees and little greenhouses full of red tomatoes. I threw myself down in the long grass, dazzled by the biggest piece of blue sky I'd ever seen. I smelt the sulphur from the engines and the scent of flowers all mixed together. I felt shaky inside. Life had changed. It was a different world and I gloried in it.

Moving into the new house improved our lot. 'Yew git a better class a' person live round 'ere,' Mum said, flinging a chenille cloth over our old scrubbed table. 'More wot I'm used to. Course, it don't suit y'r Father. 'E's like a duck out a' water wi' ed-jicated people.'

Dad was uneasy, but mainly about the garden. The neighbours' backyards flourished with cabbages, rhubarb, spuds and livestock. 'That blummin' cockerel next door gi'mme the pip, a-crowin' fit ter bust fuu'st thing of a mornin',' Dad complained.

'I in't never 'eard no cockerels a-crowin',' Mum said. She slept through until ten. We got ourselves off to school.

It was a thriving, noisy little street. Dogs barked, cats hissed, birds squabbled and shouldered each other off the branches. Men came round crying: 'Shrimps, cockles, fresh fish, winkles.' There were cries of 'horse-muck' as well, and the newspaper man passed by croaking: 'Bee-par bee-po.' He had an impediment and we copied him, then ran off and hid.

I fed my rabbits, a pair of Angoras squatting on their backsides and chewing all day. Mum combed great wedges of fur from their coats. She stuffed her old stockings with it and made draught-stoppers. She lay them down inside the door. It made you jump when you opened it and saw them, just as though Mum's legs were spreadeagled on the floor.

'They don't look up ter much, but they keeps the whool 'ouse warm,' she claimed.

When Dad was in a temper, he kicked one of these plump stockings and Mum roared out in pain. 'Yew spiteful ole sod, I felt that!'

Dad was so surprised he calmed down. 'Well, I'll be buggered,' he mumbled, 'whatever next?'

'I'll tell you what's next,' Mum said, in a good mood. 'We're goin' ter the pictures after tea. I sold some a' my eggs terday an' I'm entitled tew a bit a' pleasure out a' the money.'

'Them chickens 'ave come in 'andy, then.' Dad stroked his chin and grinned at us. 'I better 'ave a shave.'

We couldn't believe our luck. It was the first time we'd ever been taken out after tea, except to Grandma's at Christmas. You could never tell when something good might happen. It all seemed to depend on Mum. She was always changing. One day in a temper, the next singing. Sometimes she'd be in bed when we got home from school, saying she was never going to get up again.

One Saturday, when Mum went to the market shopping, Dad and I got into conversation. 'Why d'you think Mum's like that?' I asked. He took his collar off and eased himself into his chair, dazed and tired from a long week's work, his sleeves rolled up showing the black hairs on his arms.

'It's 'er moods,' Dad explained. 'Them wot 'as moods is 'ard fer others ter put up with.' I felt sorry for the way Mum treated him. First she said he wasn't a man. Then she told him off because he *was* a man and men were no damn good. Other times she flew off the handle because *she* wanted to be like a man and go out to work and not have to be a skivvy.

Dad didn't say much, but he knew everything. He knew what made people act the way they did. Because Dad liked me, he wanted to teach me things.

I was keen on getting to know everything myself. I was always ready to go down the Free Library with Mum. I took out books by Rider Haggard, H. G. Wells, Edgar Allan Poe. Mum got out books as well; Marie Corelli, Ethel M. Dell, the Baroness Orczy adventures. I read her books when I'd finished mine. At night in bed, a lot of ideas went through my head. I thought of getting up a secret society with the three girls who lived in our street. I puzzled over a name for it, and hit on The Fertile Four. It sounded important, though I didn't know exactly what it meant.

We held our first meeting in Dora's father's shed. 'Resolution Number One,' I said, 'to communicate by a secret code. Number Two. To be fertile.'

'Whatever does that mean?' Pamela interrupted, pulling her fringe down so she could hardly see. She did this when she was worried. Her hair was limp and greasy and her ears stuck out through it like a gnome's. She rubbed them because they itched.

'It means having a fertile brain, full of good ideas,' I explained.

'Oh,' said Norma, feeling her gumboil with her tongue. We all had bad habits we tried to break, but it was hard. Dora bit her nails down to the quick. I snuffled, because I had a stuffed-up nose.

'Number Three,' I went on reading them out of my school exercise book. 'To earn some money and put it in the kitty.'

Everyone looked thoughtful. Dora rubbed her nose. It had a bump in the middle. Pamela bit the inside of her lips. 'We could sell some of our clothes. The ones we don't like!' she chirped. Her hair bounced about on her head as she got excited. It was full of electricity.

'My gran wouldn't 'ave that,' Norma said, scratching her chilblains. Her hands were chapped and her knees were bony and pointed, but her blue eyes were sharp and knowing.

'Well,' I said, watching their faces, 'I think we ought to get up a play and charge people to come in and see it. I don't mind making it up, so long as no one interferes.' I already knew what it was going to be about, Lillian and Kenneth, the young doctor and his wife who had taken over at the surgery.

But when I read it out, Dora said: 'Thaa's too sloppy by a long chalk. 'Sides, I'm not goin' to be the man and put that Brylcreem on. My Mum'd go squiffy.'

I sighed. 'I wish I hadn't troubled to write it then.'

'I reckon it's good,' Norma said, 'I vote we have it.'

'Practice tonight after school in Dora's shed,' I wrote in code. 'Pass it on.' The code consisted of taking the last part of every word and putting it in the front, then adding an 'f'.

We all turned up, with some of our mother's clothes in brown paper bags, hoping they wouldn't be missed. In the first scene Lillian had to cook, while Doctor Kenneth smoked and read the newspaper. After that they went to bed. Kenneth had to undress Lillian and kiss her madly.

'We ought to have lipstick on,' Dora said.

'And eyeblack and rouge,' I said.

'What about powder and scent?' asked Pamela.

Next day Dora brought a whole box full of make-up. 'Wherever did you get this?' we gasped, full of excitement.

'I opened my money-box,' she explained with a blush. 'All right,' I said, 'let's put it all on.' I drew slanting eyebrows on Dora, like Anna May Wong in *Dr Fu Manchu* and covered up her pimples with Tokalon vanishing cream. 'You look a treat.'

Togged up in hats and long gloves, we did the play. It was called 'Doctor Incognito'.

'I know what yew lot are up to in Dora's shed,' my brother said, 'an' I'm goin' to tell Mum. You're playin' rude, in't yew?'

'If yew tell Mum, I won't do your sums any more.'

Dennis wasn't the only one spying on us. One day, as I crept out of Dora's shed, I bumped into her Dad. He was hiding behind the wheelbarrow. I tried to dodge round him, but he caught me and squeezed me hard against his chest. His face was burning and the prickles in his chin dug into my cheek. 'Put me down, Mr Foley,' I pleaded. He dumped me on the ground and strode away. I ran home crying, but I dried my eyes on Mum's silk nightdress, which I had wrapped up for the play. She wouldn't believe me if I told her what Mr Foley had done. She worshipped him because he was a true Christian and preached on Sundays at the chapel. He was Mum's idea of a real gentleman.

'There in't nuthin' that man can't dew,' she often said to Dad, 'yew've got to admit it. 'E c'n drive a motor, talk nice, keep 'is garden tidy an' allus look clean.' Dad just grunted.

Mum put the winkles on the plates and got out the pins. 'I'm not hungry, Mum,' I said. Dora had stuffed us with Mars Bars and Caley's chocolates. Her money-box must have been full. I hoped her Mum wouldn't twig.

That was why I was so worried when I came home from school and heard Mr Foley talking to Mum. I peeped in quietly; he was holding his head in his hands and tears dropped on to his chalk-striped trousers. Someone must be dead. Perhaps it was Dora's Mother. I dared not ask.

'Well, Mr Foley,' Mum said, handing him a cup of tea and a short cake, 'I ask Gal Audrey where all them sweets was a-comin' from. She told me Dora 'ad saved up the money.'

Mr Foley straightened up and blew his nose like a trumpet. His eyes were bloodshot. 'If only someone had just given us an inkling,' he said peevishly. He bit into the short cake, then put it down again. It was last week's baking. 'My wife always kept her purse in a special place on the mantelpiece. We thought it was the milkman, then we accused our charlady. To think it was our own daughter! That's what comes of letting her go to the council school. I was against it from the start. That's where she's picked up these habits, no doubt.'

Mum frowned. 'Well, Mr Foley,' she said, laying the law down, 'both a' my children goes ter the council school, but I in't never known eether one of 'em ter pinch nothin'.'

Mr Foley clasped Mum's hand and stared into her eyes. 'Oh, Mrs Emms, I didn't mean that. I just don't know what I'm saying, I'm so upset.'

'There, there,' Mum said, 'course yew didn't, Mr Foley.' She took her hand away and took her beads off the shelf and fastened them round her neck.

After Mr Foley had left, I heard Mum and Dad whispering in the kitchen. I wasn't supposed to know anything about it. But I was scared at what might happen to Dora. She was one of the Fertile Four, after all. And what about the play?

When she didn't come to school, I plucked up courage and knocked on her door. Her Mum opened it an inch or two, then stared down at me, her face pinched up and spiteful. 'What do you want?' she snapped.

'Can Dora come out to play?' I said, in a high babyish voice, as though I was an idiot. She mustn't think I knew anything.

'No, certainly not.' She began to close the door.

'Why isn't she at school, Mrs Foley?'

'We've taken her away. She's not coming to your school any more.' She slammed the door in my face. I walked home slowly, trying to think what to do. The Fertile Four was finished. Perhaps it could be the Thriving Three instead.

Dora had disappeared. It was the talk of the school. Then we forgot it. One afternoon, coming out of school with the Thriving Three, we spotted Dora. She was in a smart red uniform, with a black velour hat with a red band on it. She was carrying a hockey stick and a new leather satchel. We ran and caught her up. 'Why don't you come out to play with us, Dora?'

'I'm not allowed to play with you,' she said, 'because you led me astray. Dad said so.' Mrs Foley came out to fetch Dora, calling her from the front gate. She went without another word to us.

7
Just One More Chance

Mum had too much energy, but Dad didn't have enough. He used it all up at work. But Mum couldn't realise it. The minute he sat down with his newspaper, she started on him.

'Yew fear to be ser languid. Yew want a dose a' Kruschens down a' yew.'

Father snarled back at her. 'Yer allus crabbin', in't yer!'

'Yer got no call ter be ser oncouth.' Her eyes sparked like electricity. 'I s'puz yew don't know no better.'

'Yew've allus got ter be beefin' at someone,' Dad said, under his breath.

'Yer tryin' ter rear me up, aren't yer? Yew wish I wun't 'ere, don't yer? Glad ter see me in my 'ole, yew'll be. Well, I'm not. I'm still 'ere. Yer got a lot ter answer for. That'll all come 'oom ter yew one day.' She nodded her head at him twice, her lips a thin line, and turned up the gas-stove to a roar. ''Sides that,' she went on, still not satisfied, 'I're got a 'andle ter me name. It's Gladys – not "d'ye hear." '

Mum and Dad always called each other: 'D'ye hear.' They never used each other's names. They would be shouting 'D'ye hear' in their graves, I thought.

Father never said 'D'ye hear' to me. He called me 'dodger', or 'pingler', or 'face'. I liked all those names and he always smiled when he said them. Mum called me 'little cat', or 'brassy 'ussy!' or 'my lady'. She only called me 'sugar' when we had company. Grandma called me 'little maid'. I liked that as well.

'I'm standin' 'ere waitin' ter 'ave a shave, in't I?' Dad said.

'I don't want a lot a' your ole tuu'st,' she snapped. 'I'm busy in this damn kitchen, a-puttin' them eggs down. Yew c'n wait. Yew've got all day ter shave.'

'I don't need tellin' twice, when I'm not wanted,' Father ground out. 'I'm goin' down the garden.'

Mother started singing in a silly, swanky voice: '*Goo-oo an' leave me, if yew wish tew, never let me crawse your mind.*' She was mocking him.

'Music!' Dad snorted, but he gave me a little grin. After all, Mum wasn't in a proper temper. He was thankful for that. So was I, especially as tomorrow was her birthday. She was a Libran, like me. I'd bought her the biggest card I could get for three-pence and I was waiting for a chance to post it, without her knowing. It had a pair of scales on it. Sitting on one side was a hippopotamus weighing itself. On the other side was a lovely red rose.

'Go an' git me a quarter a' Blue Bird tuffees, Gal Audrey.'

I got on my fairy cycle and pedalled down to the post office. I popped my card in the pillar box and bought the toffees. Then a terrible sensation came over me. It was so bad I could hardly breathe. I hadn't written the address on Mum's birthday card! I chased into the post office leaving my bike on the path. The counter was very high and no one noticed me standing there.

A lady who was waiting to be served asked: 'What do you want, my beauty?' I told her what had happened and she told the man. They both glared at me.

'There in't nothin' we c'n dew about that. Yew'd 'ave ter see the Head One an' 'e's on 'oliday. Yew'd better wait outside the box till the chap come an' empty it.'

It was getting late. I leaned against the pillar box. Then I sat down on the path. After a long while the postman came and opened the box with a clang. 'Please mister,' I said, 'can you give me back my Mum's birthday card? I forgot to put the address on it.'

He was a short man with a bushy moustache and a red face. 'What d'ye take me for,' he shouted, 'a blummin' sortin' office? I in't got no time fer that sorta' caper. Once yew put that letter in the box it don't belong ter yew no more. It belong to the G.P.O.'

'But it'll never get there,' I moaned, nearly crying. I'd spent everything in my money pig, so I couldn't buy another card.

'Thaa's your look-out,' he snapped.

Mum flew out and grabbed the sweets when I got home. 'Yew little cat,' she stormed, 'wherever 'ave yew bin? I're bin all on thorns. I don't know what I're done ter deserve a gal like yew. Yew make me that dis'eartened.'

It was no good trying to explain. I put my bike in the shed and watched Dad feeding the chickens.

''Ello, dodger,' he said, 'she din't 'alf create about them sweets. Wherever'd yew git to?' But I hung my head. Then I found Minnie and cried into her fur. She didn't mind; she just purred.

'Come yew on in an' give me a 'and, Gal Audrey,' Mum bawled. I dried my eyes and went in. There was a lovely smell in the kitchen. 'I'm givin' a party fer me birthday,' Mum crammed some odd bits of pastry into her mouth. She handed me the pudding basin. 'Beat up a couple a' them eggs.' I broke one carefully, watching the yolk slosh down heavily, the white clinging to the edges.

'Git on with it, slowcoach. Yew'll git it down a' yer quick enough when it's done. Course, I'm flyin' in the face a' fortune, avin' a party. I 'ope I sh'll come orf better than I did last time. I vowed I'd never 'ave another.'

'Why was that, Mum?'

'Well, it were like this.' Mum kicked the back door to and slurped her cup of tea. 'I once give a party fer all on 'em. About ten o'clock that night, I missed y'r father. I say ter me brother Bert, "Wherever's Charlie got to?" Course, 'e bust out a-laughin'. "Waa's the game?" I ask.

' "'E's unly gone out the back," Bert say. "I'm goin' after 'im then," I say. "No, 'e's not," 'e say, "'e's in the closet."

' "I'll 'ave a look fer meself," I say. It were pitch dark in the backyard, an' I cuu'n't see where 'e were. Then I 'ear someone a-gigglin'. And wot dew yew think 'e were up to? A-runnin' round a' that backyard after an ole tart, 'e were, wi' 'is shirt 'angin' out. Talk about a sketch.

' "Come yew on 'ere, yew frisky ole bugger," I say, "I'll larn yew." But he dodged out a' me way.

'Direckly I got indoors me brother Bert say: "Did yer catch ole Charlie then?"

' "Catch 'im," I say, "I'll knife 'im, if I do." My brother give a grin. "'E's a rummun, that Charlie. The quiet ones is allus the worst! That mawther out there is my gal Mabel. We wus both out the back with 'er. I put my 'an' up 'er clo'es and there was another 'and up there as well. We both shook 'ands under 'er skirt. When I look up ter see 'oo it were, I see ole Charlie a-standin' there!" '

Mum stopped eating and ground her teeth at the shame of it. 'That did it. Thaa's the finish of 'im, I say. Let 'im find 'isself another ole tart, 'e's not a-comin' ter bed with me no more. I'm not 'avin' me nose a-rottin' orf a' me face threw catchin' diseases orf a' dirty ole men!'

I whisked the eggs with my fork, without looking at Mum's face.

'A' course, yew know nothin' about them sort a' things at yore age,' she said. 'I prayed ter God ter take all me feelin's away from me, wot I felt fer y'r father. I say ter meself, no, I say, I'm not a-sleepin' with 'im no more, I'm 'avin' them twin beds.

'My Mother she say: "Yew'll see what yew'll do, Gal Gladdy, yew'll 'ave your revenge, but yew'll dew yerself 'arm an' all. God say: Revenge is mine. I will repay. It's not up to sich as us ter take it on ourself. 'Sides, yew can bet pore ole Charlie were 'alf cut an' din't know what 'e were a-doin' of.'' So I thought it over, an' now I'm 'avin' another party. I'm givin' 'im one more chance afore I gits them single beds.'

I pelted home from school without stopping. As soon as I opened the back door, I burst out crying. Mum was doing the washing; it was one of her days when she was behind-hand because she couldn't get up.

'My stars, Gal Audrey, whatever's up wi' yew?' she bawled.

'That Miss Willett slapped me. Look at my 'ands.' I held them out to Mum. They were red and swollen. Mum's were red as well from the hot water. She wiped them on the curtains.

'Come yew 'ere, my lady,' she scowled, 'let me 'ave a look at them 'ands.' She turned them over. The backs were covered in scratches. 'Your blasted teacher did that?' Mum's cheeks flamed and her eyes flashed. 'Whatever for?' She glared into my tearful face. 'I want the truth, mind.'

'I was talking,' I admitted, downcast.

'Well, thaa's no reason for injuries like this, damn stingy beggar.'

'She's got them long nails like Anna May Wong,' I sniffed.

Mum's eyes gleamed. 'I reckon I'll 'ave ter see inter this. These 'ands could lead ter trouble. Specially if they fester, yew c'd git information settin' in. Wot time dew that school shut?'

'They'll be goin' home soon,' I said, glad to be the centre of attention.

'I'll git my coat on, then.' Mum plodded into the front-room and came back, holding her brown coat with the moth-eaten fur collar. She pulled off her stockings with the holes in and put on some with ladders in. 'Course, we was never allowed ter talk neether, when I were at school. I was unly too pleased when I could git there. My mother kept me at 'oom ter dew 'er wark, emptyin' the slops, lightin' the copper, manglin'. I 'ad ter leave altergether when I were ten.'

She searched for her face in the cracked glass over the sink, then smoothed down her frizz and jammed her hat on the top. 'Where's my blummin' shoes got to?'

I hunted under the table where she had kicked them. One was lodged under the table leg. I levered it out. The sides were all slack and the toes bulged to make room for her bunion. They looked fit for the bin. She squashed her feet into them and buttoned up her coat purposefully over her blue pinafore. You could still see it hanging down underneath.

'I was mad on '' 'Iawatha.'' Soon's ever my teacher finished the recitations, I got in a temper and shouted, "Don't stop, Miss. I loves 'earin' ' 'Iawatha'." "I'll report yew, Gladys," she say, "it's rude an' oncouth ter shout." '

She steered me up the garden path in front of her, one hand digging into my shoulder. I hung back, realising what I had done. 'Come yew on, my lady.'

'What about the rabbits, Mum?' I asked as she stalked past their hutch.

'They c'n 'ave their grub afterwards. I want ter take that bitch ter do afore she go 'oom.' Her mouth was set in a straight line. 'Let's 'ave another look at them scars.'

The scratches had faded a bit by now, so I had to keep on digging my nails in, to keep them fresh. I kept them in my pockets. I knew Mum was looking forward to a set-to. I couldn't let her down now.

' "Barb'ra Freitche", that was another one I liked. But best of all was "Excelsior". That were very dramatick! *A banner with a strange device: Excelsior!* she quoted in a deep baleful voice. 'Yer see, I can still say it,' she said proudly.

'We 'ad teachers wot were spiteful an' all,' she snapped. 'That make my blood boil; when I think on it.' But she was smiling, nevertheless.

Getting up steam, she tore along past the reservoir, crossed the road and pushed straight through the swing doors, while I nipped in behind her. I cringed as the doors smashed against the walls. Old Mr Longjohn, our caretaker, was stumbling towards us, heaving a pail of water and a mop. He dumped it down the minute he saw Mother coming and it sloshed all over the corridor, leaving a strong smell of Lysol. 'Hold yew hard, missus,' he burst out through his straggly moustache. 'Whaa's all this commotion?'

Mother ignored that. 'Oo's the 'ead one 'ere?' she bawled, 'thaa's 'oo I want ter see, not yew!' Her hat was on one side and her eyes were narrow as gimlets. He didn't argue, just pointed to the office.

It was locked. With both fists clenched, Mother beat on the door. It snapped open quickly, causing her to lurch inside. My headmistress stood there, with her mouth open. Before she could utter a word, Mother grabbed my hands and held them out in front of her, dragging me with her.

'Look at them 'ands!' she shrieked. 'My Gal Audrey's bin mauled by one a' your teachers. I'd like ter know 'zackly wot's going on in this school. Thaa's physical cruelty, that is!' Mother's spit sprayed all over Miss Hyatt.

Miss Hyatt patted the braided earphones over each side of her head. I'd often wondered how she could hear properly, but she had no trouble hearing Mum. 'And who do you think you're talking to, Mrs Emms?' She looked down her long nose at Mother, not realising who *she* was talking to. It was enough to land her up in hospital.

Luckily the door opened then and someone stalked in. It was my teacher. She'd got herself up in a smart ice-blue coat and hat, with a fox fur staring over one shoulder with its glass eyes. She thought a lot of herself. Mother recognised her instantly and turned on her with full fury.

'Yer the one I want ter see. Not 'er!' she thundered. 'Yew spiteful cat. Wot dew yew mean by layin' inter my Audrey, like that? Look at them 'ands! I'm takin' 'er straight ter my doctor ter show 'im them injuries. Then I'm orf up the Ed-jication Committee ter make a complaint against yew, an' this school! I'll 'ave yew out a' this job. Yew'll see! Yer not goin' ter treat a child a' mine like that.' Mum raised her fist.

Miss Willett opened her mouth to speak, weighed Mother up and thought better of it. Instead, she burst into tears. This took me by surprise. Surely she wasn't that scared! Miss Hyatt rushed forward with the best chair that had a red cushion on it.

'Sit down, Miss Willett, I'll deal with this! Mrs Emms, kindly keep your voice down. You're talking to one of my staff.'

Mother squared up to her. 'Don't yew dare rile me up, yew dried-up ole maid, dew I'll shoot yew over that rezie-voyer outside. I wants ter know ezackly why she made them whales on my Audrey. I intend to git ter the bottom a' this. She's a callous bitch an' shuun't be exposed ter children.'

'The girl's always talking in class, she's a chatterbox,' Miss Willett moaned in a high-pitched voice, dabbing her eyes with a posh handkerchief no bigger than a stamp.

'Thaa's no good reason ter injure 'er though, is it?' Mum bawled.

'Mrs Emms,' the head interrupted with a certain amount of pluck, 'I will deal with my staff, not you.' She wasn't in charge for nothing, but she didn't know Mum had once tamed a bull that had strayed into the butcher's shop in Ber Street, on its way to the Cattle Market.

'All right, then deal with 'er. If not, I will, an' blummin' quick too.'

'Please calm down, Mrs Emms. Miss Willett has been under considerable strain recently, due to certain private affairs.'

'Wot private affairs?' Mum snorted. But curiosity took over. 'I'd like ter know what they are.'

'It's none of your business!' screamed Miss Willett. She was getting hysterical and practically blind, with her glasses steamed up.

'I cannot discuss it here,' the head snapped.

'Oh, can't yer,' snarled Mum, 'I'll ferret this out, if it's the last thing I dew. I'm not 'avin' snakes pretendin' ter be teachers in this school.'

Seeing she meant business, the head changed her tactics. 'Well, it's like this, Mrs Emms,' she said in a sensible voice, kowtowing to Mum now. 'Miss Willett was planning to get married in a fortnight's time and now her young man has unfortunately disappeared. You'll understand her distress.'

'I don't blame 'im one bit,' Mum said, 'with a temper like she're got. But she's not takin' out 'er spite on my child. I'm not 'avin' that. Yer'll see what I intend ter dew. I'm takin' 'er away from this school, fer a start.'

Mum turned on her heel and marched out, one arm round my shoulders. She took it away as soon as we were in the street.

'Keep yore mouth shut in future,' she snapped, 'see wot a lot a' trouble yer caused through talkin' too much.' But she didn't say anything else and I could tell she was in a good mood. As soon as we got in she took her hat off and started humming: 'Smile, damn you, Smile'. Then she gave me some extra greens for my rabbits.

Mum wasn't up when I tiptoed out to school in the morning, so nothing was said about taking me away. Miss Willett wasn't there to call the register; we had another teacher instead. Everyone was excited, whispering and shuffling their feet.

Miss Walters had soft brown hair and a pleated skirt. There was a bunch of bluebells on her desk, with sticky stuff oozing out of their stalks. She picked them up, smelt them and started putting them in a vase. They were the same colour as her eyes.

'Please Miss,' Pamela put her hand up, 'where's Miss Willett got to?'

'I'm sorry to say that Miss Willett won't be coming back this term. She's had a nervous breakdown, unfortunately,' Miss Walters said. 'Now get on with your work, children, we've got lots of interesting things to do. As soon as sums are finished, I'm going to take you all out for a country walk, to study the wild flowers growing round here.'

'Coo, miss,' we chorused, pleased as punch. No one was sorry to see the back of Miss Willett. She was always laying into someone.

When Miss Walters collected our books, I had a good look at her hands. They were freckled, with short, pink nails. I looked at my own hands, turning them over in wonder. The marks that had been there yesterday had completely vanished.

Gracie wore her plainest clothes for chapel, brown lisle stockings, black lace-ups and a navy nap coat. Her velour was pulled down over her eyes and her nose stuck out underneath. But Mum dressed me in Shirley Temple style, with pretty ankle-strap shoes, even though they were scuffed.

While Gracie waited impatiently for me to get ready for chapel, I admired myself in the glass over the fireplace, standing on the stool.

'You haven't got any knickers on, Audrey Emms!' Gracie said, scandalised.

'There's no need to be so nosy, Gracie Ramsey,' I snapped. ''Sides, I'm waitin' for Mum to give me my clean ones, so there.'

The lavatory door slammed – Mum waddled out in her curlers and her pink nightgown, torn under one arm. 'I've 'ad a relief,' she sighed.

'You look worn-out, Mum,' I pandered. Mum liked people to say things like that to her. It gave her an excuse to go right back to bed. It was only nine, early for a Sunday. 'Why don't you go back to bed, Mum?'

'I'm not up yit, am I?' she snorted, plodding towards the stairs.

Gracie sniggered; her eyes glittered. Sloe-eyes, Mum called them. 'Mrs Emms,' she bleated, 'Audrey hasn't got any knickers on.' Gracie wouldn't put it past me to go to chapel without any.

Mum halted in her tracks. 'Knickers! Knickers! Wot dew I know about knickers!' she bawled. 'She's eight-year-old an' ought ter know where 'er knickers are, don't she? Where'd yer leave 'em yistiddy?'

'Under the bed,' I murmured, 'but they're gone and I can't find them now.' It was a lie. They were on the floor in Bangy Reynold's shed. We'd been playing mothers and fathers on Saturday night when Mum and Dad were at The Cherry Tree. 'Where's my clean ones, Mum?' I wheedled.

'I don't know nothin' about clean ones. It's washday termorrer, not terday, an' y'r father's too damn lazy ter mend that mangle fer me.' She glared hard at me. 'Yer'll 'ave ter 'ave yore petticuu't pinned up atween yore legs, my lady. I'll git a safety.'

Gracie's mouth hung open. We were both thinking about the pin coming undone. 'She can't come to chapel like that, Mrs Emms,' Gracie whispered, scared to argue outright. 'It'll chafe her.' I shuddered. 'I know, Mrs Emms, I've got a clean pair in my drawer I can lend her.' She shot out of the door, slamming it hard.

'That Gracie Ramsey. She'll 'ave the whool 'ouse wook up at this time of a Sunday mornin' when we sh'd all be fast asleep.' Mum opened the door and closed it again quietly, cancelling out the bang. She glared at me again. 'My heart alive, my lady, yew in't done yore 'air, 'ave yew, an' yore face is filthy.' She raked through my tangled curls with a big chromium comb. Half the teeth were bent and there was black jam between them.

'Oh, oh!' I screamed, 'don't, Mum!' I felt the tears pricking. My scalp was on fire.

'Shut yew up!' Mum got the flannel, spat on it and rubbed it hard all over my face. If I hadn't closed my eyes, she would have gouged them out. 'There y'are! When I were yore age I 'ad ter take the breakfuu'ses up ter me Mother an' Father of a Sunday mornin'. Bacon, eggs an' fried bread. An' a damn good 'idin' if it weren't jus' right. Yew don't know nothin' ter what I did.'

Dad banged on the ceiling from his bed. 'Wot's up wi' yew?' Mum shrieked, 'stop that bangin'.'

'Where's the blummin' paper?' he shouted.

Mum drew herself up and bawled. 'Up my arse, yew c'n see the end 'angin' out.' That shut Dad up. She handed me the *Sunday Pictorial*. 'Take that up tew 'im.'

All I could see of Dad was his nose. He was wrapped up tight in the counterpane. The curtains were drawn and there was a smell of feet. 'Whatever's goin' on in this damn 'ouse this morning, Gal Audrey?'

'Nothin',' I sniffed. 'Why?'

'Don't be cheeky.'

He flicked through the paper and stopped to stare at a lady in shorts and a suntop kissing a little dog and crushing it against her big chest.

'*Princess Marina and her beloved pom,*' I read out, over Dad's shoulder. 'What's a pom?'

'A pom? Well, it's a pedigree. A Pomeranian, to be exact. It's a pug, like a Pekingese, long ears and them protrudin' eyes. All they do is eat an' breathe. They're too high-bred f'r anythin' else.' He eyed me curiously. 'An' why've y'r got that flimsy frock on for?'

'I'm goin' ter chapel with Gracie Ramsey.'

'Lot a' good that'll dew yer.' Dad didn't believe in God. He was a heathen. I heard Mum say so. 'Yew wait till yew die,' Mum had shouted at him, her eyes big and threatening, 'then yew'll see where yew'll go to!'

'Strike a light!' he'd answered, 'I know where I'll be goin', in a nice big 'ole in the ground an' lay there till I rot, I dessay.'

'Yer a wicked man, an' God'll smite yer.' Mum had spoken through clenched teeth.

''E'll smite yew an' all,' Dad had been quick to say.

'Thaa's what yew'd like,' Mum had wailed back at him. 'But God know different ter that. 'E say in the Bible, "some shall be taken an' some shall be left." I'll be one a' them that's left!' That had put a stop to Dad's blaspheming.

I left Dad with his paper and went downstairs again. Gracie had brought the knickers for me. Navy-blue interlock. You could see them through my dress. It spoilt everything.

'Come on, we'll be late,' she hissed.

'Fare ye well,' Mum croaked, locking the door behind us.

We scampered past Bangy Reynold's house giggling. He ran out, pulling up his trousers. Bangy was only nine, but he was in long-uns, on account of the work he did for his Dad, which was collecting horse-muck round the streets.

'I got suffin' fer yew, Gal Audrey,' he shouted. My knickers came flying over the hedge.

'Where can I put them?' I wailed. Gracie squashed them into her coat pocket and we ran all the way to chapel. It was full up when we got there. Her Dad stood outside shaking hands with stragglers. He was the parson.

'Minister, not parson,' Gracie corrected me. 'Yew don't have parsons at chapel. 'Sides he's a *lay* minister, not a real one.' We crept into a pew and I kept out of Mr Ramsey's way. I'd never told Mum, but once he had put his hand between my legs and I'd screamed and bitten his arm.

Mum always said: ''E's very refined, that Mr Ramsey, 'e allus takes 'is 'at orf when 'e see me a-comin'. 'E's wot I call a gentleman.'

''E's what I call a snake,' Dad had snorted, 'unly yew can't see it!'

I opened my hymn book and put it in front of my face. A little man with glasses and a bald head was playing the organ, rocking himself back and forth. Everyone eyed each other's clothes, adding up what they must have cost. Gracie's Dad wore a hacking jacket and a stiff collar to keep his head well up. He bowed to the congregation and said: 'The first hymn is Number Seven: *Washed in the Blood of the Lamb.*' He led the singing in a booming voice. 'In the blood, in the blood, we are washed in the blood of the Lamb.'

The idea of it made me feel sick. To make things worse, there was a hand-painted picture on the wall of a pretty white lamb sucking on a feeding-bottle being held out by a little Indian girl.

Apart from that picture, the chapel was bare. No candlesticks, no cross, no pretty glass windows like they had at St Julian's where I used to go. Just wooden pews and scrubbed floorboards that scratched your knees.

No wonder Mum said they didn't hold with fripperies, 'them Methodis's'.

When the plate came round, I ducked my head and let it pass, holding my farthing tight. I could get five aniseed balls, or a coconut mushroom with it.

'Put your money in the collection, Audrey Emms,' Gracie hissed.

'I've lost it,' I fibbed. Then Mr Ramsey looked straight at me and said: 'Liars shall be held upside down in a cauldron of boiling oil.'

He couldn't have meant it though, because after the service was over, he came up to me smiling. 'Hello, Audrey, how's your Mum?'

'None too cracky,' I said, pulling Gracie by the hand to come home.

'Sorry to hear that. I'll give her a look in tomorrow. What time does your Dad get home?'

'Tea-time,' I said, before I had cottoned on, then I bit my tongue.

It was raining outside, splashing on the concrete in the chapel yard. A tall lady in a picture hat with a floppy brim came up to us. 'Hello Gerry,' she said to Gracie's Dad. 'Lovely service.' I was struck dumb, then I got the giggles.

'Is that your Dad's real name, Gerry?' I grinned. 'That's what we call Mum's chamber!'

I ran all the way home from the chapel, leaving Gracie behind. I couldn't stop laughing.

Next Sunday, I got up early and went to St Mark's Church instead. You could get a penny a week for being in the choir there. As I passed Gracie's house I saw her standing outside waiting to go to chapel. I burst out laughing and she ran indoors without even speaking to me.

8
The March of Progress

'My heart alive! Waa's all this muck yer fudgin' about with on my table?' Mum barked. The puppy-dogs printed on her shantung frock seemed to join in. Dad looked up into her angry face with a dreamy expression. He was in another world; the world of science.

'Why, thaa's not muck ezackly.' He put down his screwdriver and pushed his cap to the back of his head. Dad always wore his cap, indoors and out, except on holiday, then he wore his boater. 'That is what you call a wireless set, or will be once I've put it tergether.' He held out a diagram covered in dots and numbers that reminded me of my snakes and ladders. A heap of screws, a coil of wire, scraps of wood and cut-out metal shapes lay in front of him.

'A wireless set!' Mum was thunderstruck. She picked up a metal cylinder and peered into it. 'An' waa's this then?'

'That's the speaker.' Dad wiped the sweat from little grooves on his forehead.

'Waddya take me for? A fule? That can't speak!' She threw it down in superstitious dread. Everyone knew we were fifty years behind the times in Norfolk, but Mum was fifty years behind that.

'Well, it's like this,' Dad explained, 'thaa's a new invention invented by Logie Baird.' He wasn't quite sure of the name, but Mum wouldn't know any different.

'Lurgie Beard? I know 'oo yew mean. 'E's that Italian one, in't 'e?'

'Thaa's right,' Dad said, puffing his chest out and making no move to clear up.

'An' 'ow long are yew goin' ter be messin' about with this damn squitt? I're got more important things ter do, like gittin' this table set.' She flung a spoonful of Mazawattee into the pot and stirred it viciously. 'Come on, Gal Audrey, stop playin' with them cigarette cards an' give me a 'and with the tea.'

As I jumped up my set of Champion Wrestlers of the British Empire flew all over the floor. 'Pick them damn things up. Yew an' y'r Father make two!'

'No need ter git ser aeriated,' Dad sighed, 'I'm finishin' it orf at work.' He stowed everything carefully back into his toolbox. The glass accumulator with the knobs on top, he stuck on the bookshelf. It was empty, because we didn't own any books.

'Now, don't yew kids touch that,' he warned, 'it's full a' acid.'

'Acid,' I gulped, 'what, like in acid drops, Dad?'

'Certainly not! It's a chemical. It can blind yer.'

I blinked hard to make sure I hadn't been blinded already. But I could still see our cretonne curtains, with the upside-down horses galloping across them.

'Wot the p'liceman!' Mum bawled. 'Acid and chemicals in this 'ouse. Yew can git that out of 'ere double quick!'

'Thaa's not doin' any 'arm. I'll put it in the shed, if you like,' Dad said.

Mum calmed down. ''Ow long afore we c'n 'ear that thing a-playin'? I like a drop a' music.' She thought it was like a gramophone without any handle.

'Why, it'll unly be a week or two afore thaa's ready ter play,' Dad grinned.

'Coo! Dad!' My face lit up. I knew what a wireless set was. We'd learnt about it at school. Just think, Dad was making one for us! I was proud of Dad. He was an electrician. He could fix up electric lights in houses where they only had gas lights before. Mum always said he was useless. But this proved he wasn't. Dad had seen the Pyri-mids in the Great War. He could even count in Egyptian: *etneen, talatta, camsa, sitta, setta* . . .

It wasn't long before Dad had the wireless set completed.

'This is the National Programme from Daventry!' A voice crackled in the earphones and bounced about inside my head. It tickled my ears so much I ripped them off, taking some of my curls with them.

'It make my ears tingle, Dad.'

'Thaa's just the oscillations,' he laughed, fiddling with wires. 'Wait yew a minute. It'll come out a' that loudspeaker. I'm just a-tunin' in.' The whole set vibrated as it whooped and whistled in agony.

'Tunin' in! What claptrap! I'll tune you in if you don't put a stop ter that row.' Mum stuck her jaw out. But Dad put his head close to the set and listened hard. The loudspeaker was inside a brown wooden box with a pattern of a sunset on the waves carved out of the front. A piece of wire gauze was stretched across it. Every time a sound came out, it rattled. Dad twirled the knobs with both hands and somehow he got hold of a lady singing, deep in her boots:

'Somewhere a voice is calling,
Over land and sea . . .'

Mum stopped beating the egg pudding and stood open-mouthed, dripping batter off the fork on to the floorcloth.

'My stars, that sound like my Mother a-singin' on there. I'd know 'er voice anywhere. Thaa's 'er fav'rit song an' all. 'Owever did they get 'er voice inter that little box, Charlie?' Mum's blue eyes were big and round as she collapsed into a chair, overcome.

Dad winked at us. 'I reckin she must 'ave come down the chimney in the middle a' the night and got inside.'

Mum glared at the fireplace. 'That she never! I left that fire in last night. She'd a' bin bahnt up.'

'That in't Nan,' my brother chipped in. 'She 'aven't got no pianner.' He had picked out the strains of an instrument in the background.

'Contradictin' me agin, Boy Denny. Yer'll git a clip a' the lug fer that!' Mum's face flushed. Sometimes she could look big and frightening, others small and kind. It was her moods that caused it, Dad said sometimes.

My brother crawled under the table. Minnie, our cat, was hiding, her fur standing on end. 'Don't yew be so shanny, Minnie,' he coaxed. Just then the wireless set started shrieking again and the cat tore out squealing.

'Whatever 'ave yew done?' Mum roared. 'Waa's wrong with that cat?'

'She c'n feel the current, thaa's all,' Dad said, keeping calm.

'Current, wot current? Yew better put a stop ter that. I don't want no currents in 'ere, dew we sh'll all wake up dead termorrer mornin'.'

'Whatever are you a-splutterin' about? That can't affect you. Cats is different. They're subjeck ter 'lectricity, in't they?'

'This is a special announcement!' The posh voice came on again and Dad turned it up quickly. *God Save the King* was being played.

'There's suffin' a-goin' tew 'appen,' Mum whispered, 'keep yew quiet.'

A gentle, quavering voice hovered in the air, unmistakably that hesitant tone belonged to only one person; the new King.

'We live in ger-wim times, but I-ay feel sh'aw th-th-that the'ee unconquer'wubble spi'wit of tha'h Bw'itish people will nev'ah fail.' It was the time of the Abdication. We had lost one king and gained another.

Mum looked sternly at Dad. 'Fancy 'earin' 'im,' she said. 'Mind yew, I liked that other King better, 'e din't 'ave no impediments.'

She went on drinking her tea, then lifted her head and sniffed very loud. 'There's a smell a' burnin' in 'ere. That damn wireless'll set fire ter this whool 'ouse an' put paid ter the lot on us. I'm gittin' out a' 'ere.' Mum grabbed her hat with the marabou trimming and shot out into the yard behind the cat.

It was a long while before anyone else touched the wireless set. It stood in the corner on top of an orange box. It had gone quiet.

'Evil-lookin' objeck,' Mum hissed, 'come yew away from that. I don't trust it. I 'ad ter git up in the middle a' the night 'cause I 'eard it a-moanin'. My 'ead's bin that muzzy ever since y'r father brought it 'ere. It'll 'ave ter go. All that current's a-gittin' inter my 'air, an' all. Look at the state of it!'

It was true. Mum's hair was all over the place. The parting had gone all crooked and when she raked through it with the big comb, it shot out at the back like the tail feathers of a duck.

'That unly want earthin',' Dad claimed. He searched for a hole in the wall, but there wasn't one. He got out his bradawl and drilled away at the window sill. He threaded a long red and black wire through it. Mum watched suspiciously. She was bathing her thumb in a pudding basin full of Milton. She had a whitlow under the nail that wouldn't heal up. She groaned as she held it under the boiling water.

'I dew b'lieve that current 'as got inter this water,' she wailed, shoving the basin away. 'Open that kitchen winder, Boy Denny. Let that current git out, dew we sh'll never 'ave no peace in this 'ouse.' Mum thought it was an evil spirit creeping about from room to room, waiting to pounce.

'Look 'ere, Gladys, there's nothin' wrong wi' that set. I'll prove it.' Dad switched on before she could stop him.

'Rey'in, foll'ewed ba'y sho'res,' a voice said. It sounded so swanky we could hardly understand what it was on about. It didn't talk anything like us.

'Waa's that, Russia?' Mum asked.

'Thaa's not Russia, it's London. They talk different up there,' Dad said.

'It don't sound nothin' like the King's English ter me. And 'ow does they know it's a-goin' ter rain, when they're stuck inside a' that box. 'Ow're they goin' ter see what the weather's like?'

Dad swallowed a chuckle and coughed instead. Mum was serious. 'Well, yer see, Gladys, they gits it writ down for 'em on a piece a' paper. It's called "the latest weather forecast". I're told yew oo'ver an' oo'ver agin, they're not in that box, they're in a broadcasting studio room up London, called Alexandria Palace.'

'Alexandria Palace, why you said that was in Egypt, not London! Yer 'avin' me on, in't yer? 'Sides, we in't 'ad no rain fer weeks, nor likely tew. Look, the sun's out.' But Mum closed the kitchen window, just the same. She plodded upstairs and came down again carrying the cross off her dressing-table. She stood on a stool and hung it on a nail over the wireless set.

'That'll put paid ter yew,' she said and started humming: 'Nearer My God to Thee'. She had a round of bread and jam in her mouth, so you couldn't hear it properly. She was getting our dinner ready and it made her peckish. She put an enamel plate on the table rattling with winkles. Shiny and black, with little lids like celluloid. Inside they were all mother-of-pearl and sweet, salty and juicy at the same time.

'Git the pins, Gal Audrey, so we c'n eat them hydroids.' I got out Mum's workbasket and laid a pin beside each plate. Mum went on slicing the bread, so I trailed outside to look for Minnie. To my horror she was in the shed, with her furry head stuck in my jam-jar, crunching up my tadpoles. She couldn't get them down quick enough. Some of them had grown legs overnight and they were sticking out from the sides of her mouth.

'Cannibal,' I yelled, and slapped her hard. She growled and crouched down. There was no sense in trying to rescue the tadpoles.

'Stingy beggar,' my brother said.

'Don't worry,' I said, turning my nose up, 'she's unly ate your half of them tadpoles, not my half. I've got mine here, see!' I pretended to hold them safely inside my cupped hands. Then I ran out of the back gate before he could catch me.

When Mum heard the gate click, she put her head out of the kitchen window and called out: 'Gal Audrey, I're got an erran' fer yew. I want yew to go round Mrs Youngman's an' ask 'er for a lend of 'er rosary. Say y'r Mum want it specially.'

''Er rosary?' I asked. 'Whatever for?'

'Never yew mind, my lady. Do wot I tells yer.'

I dawdled past the backyards till I got to Youngmans' house. I didn't know what she would say. Mrs Youngman was Mum's friend. Once she'd given me a pair of grey silk stockings with only two ladders in them. I was keeping them in my bottom drawer, with the pink garters my Auntie had given me. I would wear them at my birthday party.

The Youngmans were having their fish-and-chips. They sat

round the table in their poky living-room with the electric light on. She came to the door, wiping her mouth on the sleeve of her old Fair Isle jersey. The hole in the front showed her petticoat. To think she had the cheek to say my brother and I were like the Bisto Kids!

''Ello, Gal Audrey, thaa's a pretty frock you're got on. Now wot can I do fer yew, my little maid?' She gave me an artful smile. Behind her tousled head I saw a picture of Jack Buchanan that she'd cut out of *John Bull*.

'Mum ask if she c'n borrow your rosary, Mrs Youngman. She won't keep it long.' I knew she'd weigh up what I said and think Mum had gone loopy and this made me feel funny and breathless.

'Come yew on in, Queenie,' Mr Youngman bawled, 'we're 'avin' our dinner, in't we?'

'It's only Gal Audrey. She want ter borrer me rosary.'

His mouth fell open, showing a mouthful of half-eaten fish-and-chips. He had his pin-striped jacket on, but no shirt underneath. I could see the hairs on his chest and it made me feel sick.

'It's gettin' overcast,' I said, trying to make conversation. I pointed to the sky over their shed, where grey clouds were scudding. 'Did you know it was going ter rain?' I asked proudly. 'We knew. The latest weather forecast from Daventry said so.'

The whole family stared at me, forks half-way to their mouths. 'I doubt it,' Mr Youngman said. They didn't know what I was talking about.

Mrs Youngman handed me a long silver chain threaded with black beads and a tiny little Jesus. ''As your Mum seen the light then?' she said gently.

'Yes,' I whispered. I was no fool. Her face cleared. 'Well I'm glad a' that, ole dear.'

It was pelting with rain as I ran home. I was in my blue slub frock, with the open-work collar Auntie had crocheted for me. The driving rain felt like needles on my back.

'Thaa's a-thund'rin' out there, Mum,' I gasped.

'Come yew on in an' wipe yore feet, my gal. An' don't go near that objeck in the corner while the storm's a-lastin', dew we'll all be electrified,' Mum warned.

'Whatever do that mean, Mum?'

'Struck down dead,' she said. 'Did yew git the rosary for me?' She stuffed it in the pocket of her dress with the little dogs on it.

'When your Grandma 'ad a crow fly down of 'er chiminey, she got 'er rosary out and put a spell on it. It fell down dead in the middle a' the floor. Thaa's wot I intend doin' wi' that contraption.'

'Oh Mum,' I said, half afraid of what she might do. But when I looked at Dad, he was laughing helplessly behind his news-paper, so I wasn't worried any more.

'It's quite 'armless,' Dad said, 'I're told yew afore.'

''Armless or not,' Mum said scornfully, 'I don't need wireless sets ter tell me waa's goin' on in the world. I can 'ear people talkin' 'owever far away they are, 'cause me ears burn. If it's something bad it's always the left an' if it's good, then it's the right. Why should I need fangled things like that?'

I got on with the washing-up. I was singing to myself:

'Coom, coom, coom, remember you're a Plum,
What's the use of worrying when things look glum?
For it doesn't matter what the weather
Plums will always 'ang together . . .'

I'd learnt it from listening to the BBC when Mum was out. I was used to switching the wireless on and off now. In time, I thought, Mum would get used to it as well.

The Goblin man took Mother by surprise. She was washing herself in the kitchen sink. She didn't hear him knock because her ears were full of soap. The back door wasn't locked and he just walked in.

''Oo are yew, comin' in 'ere like this?' Mum roared. She faced him full tilt in her pink petticoat with a large expanse of soft white flesh showing. The Goblin man shrank back.

'Well, I'm very sorry, missus, I'm sure, but I must be in the wrong 'ouse.' He lifted his hat and closed the door again. Then he stood outside and called through a crack in the window. 'I've got something for you, missus.'

Mother opened the window and threw her flannel in his face. 'Git yew out a' my yard,' she bawled, 'or I'll take my short-brush ter yew.' Mother's short-brush was an object of dread. She battered the carpet and the coconut matting and my brother and me with her short-brush. That is, if she could catch us.

The Goblin man persisted. 'I represent the Goblin people an' I've brought you one of our new-style vacuum cleaners, free of charge,' he shouted through the letter-box.

Mum was taken aback. A vacuum cleaner, fancy that! She'd always wanted one. She couldn't resist it. 'Give us a minute,' she called, 'till I git suffin' on. You *would* come when I'm stripped, wouldn't yew.'

In the heat of the moment she grabbed her best apricot

blouse with the scalloped cape and dolman sleeves. She ran a comb through her hair and rushed to the door.

'Pleased to meet you,' the Goblin man beamed.

'That's quite all right,' Mum said.

He had a natty little moustache and an appealing grin, but pointed ears that stuck out from his head. He was well turned out in a green Harris tweed jacket and co-respondent shoes with tapered toes. Mother was so impressed she let him in.

'Wipe your feet,' she cautioned, 'I just done my floors.'

'You needn't a' done them. This little gadget'll do the lot in no time, with no effort on your part, my dear.'

'Well, I don't mind tryin' it if it's free, but I'm not givin' it 'ouse-room, if not. My 'usband'd skin me alive if I signed up fer anything.'

'Wot, a lovely young lady like you! I sh'd think you'd twist 'im right round your little finger,' he said.

Mum simmered down. 'My stars, don't talk ter me about 'im. 'E gi'mme the 'ump. Once 'e's finished 'is day's wark, 'e in't fit fer nothin' else, 'cept sittin' in that chair a-readin' 'is *Daily 'Erald*.' She patted the back of her hair and rolled her eyes.

The Goblin man gave her a sidelong glance. 'If I was in your shoes missus, I'd give 'im something ter make 'im stir his stumps, lest you'll give 'im the push.'

'Yew wouldn't talk ter my 'usband like that, dew you'd git a ding acrawse the chops,' Mum said.

The little man dragged a big box inside and put it in the middle of the living-room. He pulled out a long steel cylinder covered in imitation leather, with a picture on the side of a goblin in a tall pointed hat with bells on it. He screwed a long metal pipe into the front and took out two attachments. 'These are the feet,' he explained, 'you c'n get up the stairs with these. Save you a lot of elbow-grease.'

Mum watched him screwing everything together, then he put his head on one side and said, 'Haven't I seen you somewhere, missus? Now let me see. It must have been down the Conservative Club. Or perhaps it's just wishful thinking.'

Mum laughed wildly. 'You wun't catch me there with all them toffs. My sirs, the Cherry Tree's more in my line.'

'Oh, so it's the Cherry Tree, is it? Now I know where to find you.'

'Shut you up,' Mum giggled. 'Let's 'ave a look at this machine a' yours when it's goin'.'

'Straightaway, my dear. I'll soon 'ave it in workin' order. Now, if you'll be kind enough to provide me with a little bit of soot out of your chimney and some of that ash from the hearth, you'll see what it can do.'

''Strewth!' said Mum, 'waddya want all that for?'

'Just throw it all down on the floor and I'll show you what'll happen. It's magic, you see.'

Mum chucked all the soot and muck over the living-room floor in no time. The Goblin man started hunting round for the plug. 'Where's the plug?' he asked, getting down on his knees in the middle of it all, careless of his nice neat plus-fours.

'Plug? Wot plug?' Mum asked. 'We in't got no plugs 'ere.'

'No plugs! We're sunk then!' The Goblin man collapsed on his heels.

Mum was thunderstruck. 'An' what about all this blummin' mess in my 'ouse then? What're yew goin' ter do about that?'

The Goblin man tried to smile, but one side of his mouth wouldn't go up properly. 'I just don't know, missus. I've never come up against anything like this before. They all have plugs. I suppose we could try the light fitment.' He hopped up on the table and took the bulb out. All at once the cleaner started up with a high-pitched whistle. The long pipe whirled round, taking on a life of its own, smashing against the walls. The soot flew up and covered the room. Mum rushed to pluck her pink knickers off the fireguard where they'd been airing.

'My stars, waa's all this? Yew'll ruin me whool 'ouse wi' that contraption. Turn that orf at once.' She couldn't hear herself speak, though she was shouting at the top of her voice. The noise was terrific.

'Never you mind, missus. I'll soon have this all ship-shape, you see if I don't. Just you go an' make us a nice cup a' tea an' I'll do all your housework for you.'

Up and down the cleaner went until everything was clean as a whistle. Mother was over-awed. 'Well, I never would 'ave credited it, if you 'aden't a' shew me,' she smiled. 'Yore welcome to a cup a' tea, but I in't got nothin' to eat. I'm on a banana diet. I'm reducin', yer see. No biscuits, no buns, only damn bananas.'

'Don't you worry about that, my dear, I always carry my own refreshments.' He switched off and emptied his pockets on to the table-cloth while Mum watched him hopefully. A few nuts and raisins, half an apple and a jam sandwich, covered in crumbs. He split it down the middle and handed her half.

'What's in it?' she asked.

'Nectar,' he said. 'I live on it.'

Mum didn't answer. Her mouth was full. 'I in't never 'ad that kind a' jam before, but it taste all right. I'll soon scorf that. I fear ter be ser 'ungry, I 'ardly know what I'm a-doin' of. I could just put paid to a couple of nice juicy chump chops, that I could.'

'Why ever don't you have 'em then? 'Oo's going ter know?'

'You're tryin' ter tempt me, in't yew, an' yew never know where it might lead to.'

'I'd like to tempt you,' he said, with an elfish grin, and chucked the cat under the chin, instead of Mum. Minnie reared up like a tiger and hissed at him, her teeth bared. He snatched his hand away.

'Wotever 'ave yew done ter that cat? 'E's allus ser meek an' mild.' Mum was flabbergasted.

'Cats don't like me much.' The Goblin man looked suddenly different, angry and misshapen. His eyes glittered. Minnie jumped off the chair and slunk through the door, flattening herself out like a shadow.

The Goblin man put his hat on. He seemed in a hurry to go. 'There's nothin' to sign. I'll leave the cleaner with you for twenty-one days on trial. You're not obliged to have it, if you don't want it, after that.'

Mum let him out. It was foggy outside and he just seemed to be swallowed up. 'Did you see 'im?' Mum said, as I walked in from school.

'Who? I in't seen no one.' Mum had a funny look on her face.

'But you must've passed 'im, the Goblin man. 'E's brought me a buckshee cleaner. Come an' 'ave a look.'

When I saw the new vacuum cleaner, I didn't know what to believe. How did she get it free? Things like that cost more than we could ever afford.

Dad didn't know what to make of it either. 'You must've signed up for it,' he said. Then he read a piece in the paper about a salesman who got fined in court for not keeping proper records of where he had delivered three vacuum cleaners, the property of the Goblin Company.

He read it out to Mum, slowly and deliberately, as though it was very important. 'That in't nothin' ter do with me, is it?' Mum said. 'The one I're got is a free sample, in a manner of speakin'. I'm not partin' with it now.' Dad didn't bother to argue. It wasn't worth it.

9
Madame Ozena's Juveniles

'That Gal Audrey's always on 'er toes. She're got dancin' on the brain. She ought ter be on the stage, an' thaa's a fack!' Mum spat on her handkerchief and washed my face with it. Her fingers dug into my shoulder as she steered me towards the lady at the piano, for my audition, that Saturday morning.

'It's in the fam'ly, a' course,' she droned on, 'my Auntie May were on the 'Ippodrome, y'know.'

I shrank back, while Madame Ozena of the Madame Ozena Juvenile Troupe summed me up with her piercing blue eyes. A little girl in a pink organdie frock, small for her age, with long dark ringlets. Mum had copied the dress from a photograph of the little Princess Elizabeth in *Silver Star*. It was like all my clothes, gaudy. They made me stand out from the others at school. But here at the dancing troupe I seemed to fit in better. The juveniles were all in frills as well.

'Go on, my lady,' Mum snapped, her jaw stuck out, her eyes like gimlets, 'dew y'r stuff!'

At the other end of the room a few little girls were rehearsing, turning cartwheels and walking on their hands. I watched them enviously.

'Can you do that?' Madame wheezed. She was a heavily-built woman, who seemed to have bad bronchitis. She wore a lovely blue velvet frock with a scalloped peplum round her middle. I noticed she didn't talk Norfolk like us. She must be from away. Away was a magic word. Away was where I wanted to be just then.

I smiled at her shyly, getting ready to say something. To my surprise, she smiled back, a twinkling smile that gave me a feeling everything was all right.

'I can do the splits,' I said, blushing because I'd spoken up.

Madame waved her fat hand. 'Come on, dear, let's see you.' I went down slowly, fingertips supporting my fly-weight body. She waited till I was down flat to the floor, then nodded her head in a business-like way. Mum was beaming at me. She patted the back of her hair, knocking her new hat with the Tudor brim askew.

'My stars!' she told Father afterwards. 'That Gal Audrey didn't 'alf speak up fer 'erself. I din't 'ave ter tell 'er wot ter say, nor nothin'.'

'Well, that's all right then, but we'll have to see what else she can do,' Madame croaked. She called to a young boy who was taking the girls through their paces in the corner. 'Come here, Stanley. We've got a new one here.'

Stanley tripped towards us. He was dressed like a lady in satin tights, but he had a little black moustache, so he must be a man. He only looked about twelve close to, but he had an old face with little red veins on his cheeks. 'This is my son,' Madame said proudly.

'She's a little minnifer, ain't she?' he said. He wasn't very big himself, I thought. He had a high-pitched voice and his hair stood up in a quiff.

'Can you sing, little girl?' he asked coyly.

'Sing! Course she c'n sing,' Mum interrupted before I could say no. 'She're got a lovely voice.'

How could Mum say that? My heart sank. I had a voice, it was true, but it was sweet and small and didn't carry far. This was a room the size of a theatre.

'All right then, come out in front and give us a song.'

Close to tears, I blundered forward. Madame Ozena raised her hands and struck up, her magyar sleeves slid back, showing her muscles. I recognised the song: 'The Quaker Girl'. Grandma often sang it. But my throat was dry and my tongue stuck to the roof of my mouth. Only the dread of what I would get when Mum got me home forced me to try and sing.

I opened my mouth and a great big voice came out of it. I hadn't noticed Stanley raise his arms towards the troupe. They had all joined in the song, linking arms and tripping round me in a circle, swishing their skirts.

*'I like your apron and your bonnet
And your little Quaker gown,
Your manners so demure
When your modest eyes look down,
And when you're walking out on Sunday
Every time I look at you,
I always think I'd like to be
A Quaker too.'*

All my shyness dropped away. I wasn't alone and frightened. I was part of all those children. We were together. For the first time, I felt free of Mother and her tantrums. I was somebody. I was one of the dancers.

'This little girl would make a lovely Dolly Varden,' Stanley patted my head. 'She's that dainty.' He balanced on his toes, as he spoke, hands on hips.

Madame eyed my skinny legs in my white socks and ankle straps. Then she said grudgingly, 'Well, she shows promise, Mrs Emms. Bring her next Saturday. Nine o'clock sharp.' She slammed the lid of the piano and changed the music.

'We'll be 'ere on the dot,' Mum smiled. She looked as though she'd just been handed a cream horn. She smoothed down the bodice of her blue moiré frock. The white jabot was spotted with grease. Madame stared at the spots. Then she fingered my curls. 'Lovely hair, Mrs Emms. Is it natural?'

Mum's cheeks puffed out with pride. It was really she who was being praised up. 'Natural? Why certainly, it's in the fam'ly, like the dancin'. I recolleck when me Auntie May . . .'

Madame changed the subject quickly. 'Now Mrs Emms, what about Audrey's costumes? Can you make things yourself, or shall we get them made up for you?'

'Get 'em made up? No fear! Why, I were apprenticed ter Chamberlains in the Market Place, where all the quality 'as their clo'es made ter measure.'

'That's handy, Mrs Emms. You might see your way to taking on a bit of sewing for the troupe, then?'

'I shuun't make no bones about that,' Mum clucked, 'provided me 'usband don't create.'

Madame and Mother stared at each other, like two tigresses stalking one another for an advantage.

'Why Mrs Emms, you're not having trouble with him, are you?' She pretended to be sympathetic, but really she was quizzing.

'Nothin' I can't 'andle,' Mum drew herself up and straightened her hat. I pictured Dad trying to put up a fight and laughed inside myself.

It was lucky he didn't because, night after night, Mum and I went off and left him to put my brother to bed. Mum lugged the big case tied up with string, with my 'Dinah' rig-out, tap shoes, ballet slippers, costumes and head-dresses.

''Urry up, Gal Audrey, dew we'll miss the charabang. 'Ave yew got your make-up?' I ran after her. I'd been staring in the looking-glass, seeing which side of my face looked the best.

The troupe was booked to perform at the village halls outside Norwich. Life in the countryside was unbelievably dreary in winter and our concerts were the big attraction for miles round.

'On stage everyone!' The curtain went up and I strutted across the boards, small and perky in my red-and-white striped costume, singing in my tinny little voice:

'Dinah, is there anyone finer,
In the State of Carolina,
If there is an' you know her,
Then show her to me.
Dinah, with her Dixie eyes blazin',
How I love to sit an' gaze in',
To the eyes of Dinah Lee.'

I waved my Al Jolson straw boater back and forth and did my tap-dance.

Madame put everything she'd got into the piano. Her whole body vibrated. Beads of sweat came out on her forehead. Her hair was thick and wavy and a soft, squirrel brown. I hadn't seen many women with wavy hair. No one could afford a perm. My aunties had straight bobs, or a bun. Mum said they let themselves go once they were married. No man wanted his wife to look like a tart, 'all geared up'. Mum used Tokalon vanishing cream on her cheeks. Nothing else. One tube lasted her a year.

I liked Madame. For all her size, she looked pretty in her lamé dresses and long ear-rings. She smelt nice too. Mum didn't hold with scent because people wore it to cover up something nasty. All you needed was carbolic and a clean smell.

Madame found out that I was comical and made people laugh. She gave me leading parts in the show and soon I lost all my shyness. Dressed up as Nelly Wallace, in a long hobble skirt and a tiny bonnet with a big geranium nodding in the brim, I tottered out from the wings. The country people clapped and cheered. 'Actions!' Madame bawled, her hands poised ready to crash down on the keys.

'Ho! 'E kissed ma,
When 'e left ma,
An' 'e told ma to be trew,
An' 'e gave ma a gerani'umm
So I'll always love yew . . .'

I hugged myself tight when I said 'kissed ma', with a little shaking movement, and pursed my lips into a big kiss. Then I wiped my eyes, pretending to be crying. I put one finger coyly underneath my chin, with eyes turned upwards for 'I'll always love you'.

'Madame reckon that Gal Audrey'll go a long way,' Mother claimed. Dad sniffed, but didn't answer.

Once the curtain went down, the whole troupe fluttered across the stage to take a bow, while someone presented Madame with a bouquet of daffs or chrysanths. She bent down low in her long velvet cloak with the white ermine collar, her diamond ear-rings swinging. It was just like a scene from *Gold Diggers of 1933* and she was the star. Stanley helped her into the Austin Seven and off they went.

After the fish-and-chips served up on newspapers, Mum went into action, throwing all the costumes into the case and staggering across the muddy field towards the coach. 'Git up the front, Gal Audrey, an' take them toe-shoes orf.'

My ballet slippers were stained with blood, where the tips of my toes had split open. 'We'll 'ave ter give them feet a good rinse, once yew gits 'ome, my lady.'

By the time we got there, more often than not it was after twelve. Dad was asleep in his armchair, with the alarm clock on his lap. He sprang up, thin strands of hair falling across his high forehead, his eyes wild. 'What time d'ye call this?'

'Waa's up wi' yew?' Mum snorted. 'We in't doin' no 'arm.'

'I'd like ter know where you've bin till this time a' night!' Dad shouted, loud for him. Mum's face changed and her eyes gleamed.

'Think I're got a fancy man, dew yew? I'm 'ot stuff, I am. Yer not jelly, are yer?'

I stared at both of them, scared she was overdoing it. Dad's face was chalk white and stiff as he moved towards her. 'If I catch yew, I'll murder yew, straight I will!' he ground out through his teeth.

She gave in then. 'Oh, dry up and let's git ter bed,' she snapped. She wouldn't tantalise him too much, in case he started making trouble. Mum was enjoying every minute of those trips out and she didn't want them to stop.

But Dad made a stand. At dinner-time next day, he coughed out loud and then spoke up. 'All this damn gallivantin', I don't like it. I tell yew straight, Gladys. It's making that Gal Audrey saucy.'

'Saucy! Saucy!' Mum yelled. 'What do you mean? That gal's just learnin' 'ow ter stick up fer 'erself, so's she'll know 'ow ter move in different circles when she's older. Thaa's more 'n you've ever done, in't it?'

Mother was full of herself that night, because the coach driver had offered her a Craven 'A' and she'd smoked it right through to the end. It was her first cigarette. Then she'd flirted with him all the way home. He was a big yokel, with his hair plastered down with Brylcreem and plenty of gumption, or so Mum had said. She was wasting her time with someone like Dad.

'See what sort of a father you've got, Gal Audrey? 'E's tryin' ter put a stop tew your dancin'.' She wanted to get me on her side. Feeling sorry for Dad, or agreeing with his point of view, meant I had betrayed her. She wanted all the love for herself, but somehow she couldn't get it.

'I can't argue with yew,' Dad said, 'yew allus 'ave ter be right, but yew may find out different.'

On Empire Day there was a fancy-dress parade and the whole street was decorated with flags of all nations. The Grint family next door had their gramophone blaring out. I put on my black patent tap shoes and tap-danced to the music. 'Why, she's the image of Janet Gaynor!' Billy Grint picked me up and carried me on his shoulders. He was a tall boy of sixteen, with crisp curly hair, just like Charles Farrell, who played opposite Janet Gaynor. After that, everyone in our street called me 'Janet' and I gloried in all the attention I was attracting.

Dad was right. I was changing. The applause had gone to my head. My photograph was in the *Evening News* when I won my diploma for dancing and musical comedy. Nothing could stop me now.

'Wake up! Wake up! Audrey Emms!' My teacher was shaking my shoulder. I rubbed my eyes and stared round the class-room. Everyone was giggling. 'That's the third time you've fallen asleep during lessons, Audrey. I'm sending you straight home today.'

I walked home, pale and tired, and handed Mum a letter from school.

Dear Mrs Emms,
I am sorry to say that Audrey is not attending properly in class. She seems tired out and keeps on falling asleep. I would suggest she is not going to bed early enough. If she does not improve perhaps you would kindly take her to the clinic for a complete overhaul.
Yours truly,
Anthea Hyatt

'I told you what you'd dew, didn't I?' Dad said slowly, folding the letter back in the envelope. 'Ruin that gal's health.'

'Yer a slink,' Mum hissed, 'spiteful and vindictive. I told yer so! I told yer so! Allus tryin' ter crow over me, aren't yer?' But she knew she was beaten. The strain of dancing and the late nights had begun to tell. I couldn't get up in the mornings. I wasn't growing as tall as the other girls of my age and I looked washed out.

How long this state of affairs might have gone on, I don't know, but a natural event intervened. My ninth birthday. It stopped the show. I was too old for the Juveniles.

I had to say goodbye to that imposing figure, Madame Ozena. Her son Stanley was just off to America to study the new dance routines. Madame bent down and I hugged her. The raddled old face was tearful and so was mine. 'You could have gone a long way, Audrey. You've got the makings of it,' she said huskily. 'Come back when you finish your schooling and we'll start you off again with my seniors, the Modernaires.' But I never did.

10
Principles at Stake

'I'll larn yer to take the juice at me.' Mother squared up to Dad, arms akimbo, voice rasping. I kept my eyes down, concentrating on my plate. Then she launched herself bodily at him, grinding her teeth, hair shooting out in all directions. I ran and cowered against the pink wallpaper with the gold hearts on it. They were a good luck charm. I pressed the backs of my hands against them, asking the fairies to put a stop to the row.

'Hold yew hard!' Father bawled, shielding his head with one arm and holding Mum off with the other. She veered round, grabbed the geranium and hurled it full into his face. He ducked and the mould showered all over the table-cloth. Our plates were full of earth. By now she was raving, her temper focused on Dad. Whatever had he done? He didn't seem to know. But he decided to beat a retreat. He pulled on his threadbare jacket and went back to work without his dinner, looking stunned. He had a two-mile walk and time to think on the way.

I started sweeping up, shaking the table-cloth in the backyard and washing up the plates. Mum threw herself into the armchair and started sobbing. Her forehead was all red. 'It's my 'ead,' she wept, 'if it don't stop painin' me, I dunno what I may do ter meself.'

The Seidlitz powders stood on the mantelpiece. I took one out and mixed it with water. ''Ave a S'idlitz, Mum,' I said.

'All this 'ousework ter dew and no one ter 'elp me,' she wailed, slurping it down noisily.

'I'll give you a hand, Mum,' I said.

'No, yew won't,' she snapped, forgetting to weep, 'yew never do nothin' right.'

After tea the doctor arrived. 'Where's your Mother, Audrey?' he asked.

'Abed,' I said. He plodded upstairs with his black case. I waited at the bottom, hoping to hear what they said.

'I'm takin' yew two up y'r Granny's,' Dad said, when he came home from work.

'Where's y'r Mother?' Grandma scowled, 'she should a' bin 'ere gittin' my tea riddy.' Dad sat down heavily and put his hands over his face. Grandma glared at him. 'Whatever's 'appened, Charlie?'

Dad cleared his throat and dabbed his eyes with the back of his hand. 'Gladys in't none too cracky. She fear ter be a bit funny. Dr Murphy come. Said it were a nervous breakdown.' Dad stared wildly round the room, from Grandma in her four-poster with the red curtain pulled to keep out the draughts, to the chenille-covered table top full of bric-à-brac, the big shiny aspidistra, the blue bird with sharp beak underneath its glass cover and the cracked cup next to Granny's medicine.

'Narvous breakdown?' she snorted. 'So thaa's wot they calls it? I never 'eard sich squit in all me life. That in't no narvous breakdown! It's 'er evil temper. She's jus' a-givin' in ter 'erself, thaa's all. She want puttin' in 'er place, if yew ask me. I 'ad ter take a stick tew 'er many a time when she were a minnifer.' Grandma's hands itched to do it again.

But Dr Murphy thought different. 'Now, Mr Emms,' he advised Dad, 'don't leave your wife all on her own. Keep young Audrey at home to look after her. She's a sensible girl.'

'She fear ter want ter dew someone some 'arm,' Dad mumbled sheepishly. 'She even threatened ter dew 'erself in, y'know.'

The doctor picked up the wedding photo on the mantelpiece. Mum in a long white dress, with her veil pulled down to her eyebrows and flowers on the top. She looked a different person. So did Dad, in a collar and tie, holding a beautiful Homburg hat on his knee.

'I'll give her a tonic. She'll soon calm down. Don't worry, man!' He snapped his bag shut, put his bowler on and went. We heard his car draw away.

My brother and I watched Dad nailing up the bedroom windows. He had tears in his eyes. Mum lay on the pillow with a white face. She took no notice of us.

Every day Dad gave us bread and jam before he went to work. Mum didn't get anything ready for us, though she got up and roamed about the house with her coat on. The cretonne curtains stayed closed.

'Whatever's the matter, Mum?' I asked, staring at her tousled hair and dirty face.

All she said was: 'Look what they done ter me. It's yer father wot set them on. 'E's took my almanack away and I can't find out what day it is.'

'It's Tuesday, Mum.' Her collar was turned up round her mottled cheeks, but she didn't intend going out, because she'd got her winceyette nightdress under her coat. Yet she had her black rubber goloshes on.

'I'm beat,' Dad said, when he came in tired out. He took his cap off, leaving a red groove across his high forehead. Then his mouth fell open. 'Where's all the pictures gone to?'

'Mum's put them in the bin,' I explained. I'd watched her squashing them down, breaking the glass and the wooden frames.

'What! Even that one with the Cathedral on it?' He marvelled over it, scratching his head as he plodded up the garden to look. He came back with a pile of clothes. 'She're put everything out a' the wardrobe in that bin.' We hid them all behind the front-room couch. No one ever went in there. There was mud on her dresses. 'That'll dry up,' Dad said. 'Nothin' fer tea, as usual, I s'puz, 'cept bread an' pull'it.'

There was a gentle tap on the back door. It was Mrs Harford, our neighbour. 'How's yer Mum?'

'None too cracky,' I said.

'Would yew two like ter come an' 'ave a bite with us?' My brother and I went with her. There was a nice fire burning and it was clean and tidy. But she gave us watercress sandwiches and it tasted so bitter, I left mine on the plate. 'Yer Mum'll be right as rain once the better weather sets in. She can't abide the cold, thaa's all it is.' She was a bushy little woman in a grey mohair cardigan with long hairs all over it. She gave us all a serviette with our tea. I folded mine up very small and put it in my pocket. The tea-cosy had a pink rosette on top and the mantelpiece had a piece of tinsel stretched across it.

'Come on, Gal Audrey, let's be gittin' 'oom,' my brother pulled my arm.

'I want to stay a bit longer. It's nice and warm here,' I said, but I had to go.

But our neighbour was right. On the first sunny day, I came home from school and heard Mum singing: 'Somewhere a voice is calling, over land and sea.' I stopped outside the door listening while she let rip. She sounded just the same as she used to be. The kitchen smelt of baking and there was a Victoria sponge on the table.

''Ello, Gal Audrey, d'ye want a bit a' sponge?' she said. Her hair was done in a lovely big wave on one side and she had on her brown bouclé frock with her court shoes. The house was tidy and some more pictures were on the walls. I noticed she was cutting the sponge with the big knife Dad had kept hidden away. 'I 'unted everywhere fer this damn knife,' she said, 'an' where d'ye think I found it? Why, on top a' the wardrobe. God know 'owever it got up there.'

But Dr Murphy told her to keep on taking the medicine. Mother found it hard to remember. She hated new habits. She liked the old ones.

'That med'cine a' stood up there over a week an' I in't touched it. I keep on meanin' to.' She nodded at the mantelpiece crowded with ornaments, matches, a comb full of hair and her Tokalon vanishing cream. 'I 'ate people rulin' me an' tellin' me what ter do. I like my own way too much.' She began explaining to Mrs Harford her way of life, while she stood there sipping her tea. Mum had asked her in for a piece of cake.

'I lays there in the mornin' till they're all gone, then I gits up. I puts me ole coat on 'cause it's perishin'. Then I sets light ter that fire. If it don't get up, I know the wind's in the east and that'll never draw.' In Norfolk the east wind is an ill wind and Mother's eyes were turned heavenwards as she spoke.

'I know what yew mean,' said Mrs Harford.

'Then I gits meself a bowl a' gruel, an' I take it back ter bed wi' the newspaper. Sometimes I dooze orf agin till about eleven, then I gits up agin an' puts the spuds on fer 'is dinner.

'Once 'e's gorn back ter wark, I strip an' 'ave a good wash in the kitchen. I tidies the 'ouse up and go down a' the market shoppin'. I gits a pint a' winkles fer tea, or some a' them chitterlin's.' They were brittle brown things like dollops of horse manure. I didn't like them.

Mum stopped for breath and rammed a slice of bread and butter into her mouth. She didn't need anyone to answer her. All you had to say was yes, or no.

It was such a humdrum existence. I never wanted to have a life like hers. I wanted to be pretty and lead an exciting life like Janet Gaynor. The neighbours said I was the image of her. I read Mum's *Silver Star* and *Woman's Friend*. I was following the serial about Madge Hildegard, the beautiful spy, who lived a double life and had countless young men in limousines waiting outside her hotel. She wore gloves with gauntlets and eye-veils on hats which were made of soft velvet and sequins. Nothing like Mum's hat when she came to meet me out of school sometimes.

She would bustle towards me and I ran to meet her. My Mum was collecting me today! But when I saw the frown on her face, I stopped running. That was on one of her unbearable days, of course. But then to us she was unbearable a lot of the time. The kitchen was always in a muddle. If I tried to get a saucer out, all the plates fell down. She crammed the cupboards full of bits and pieces. She was always losing everything and accusing us of stealing her things. She was engrained with prejudice and superstition.

'Me 'and 'as bin itchin' all the mornin',' she said, 'so I knew I'd be 'anded some money. Then y'r Father come in with that two shillin's fer them eggs 'e sold down a' the firm. It's a sure sign. If it's the left 'and yew give and the right 'and yew take.' You couldn't argue with Mum. She knew she was right. 'Me Mother were 'zackly the same, it's heerie-dittary, the second sight. She read the teacup like a book. She 'ad pree-m'nitions. Whenever 'er feet itched, she knew she were goin' on strange ground. She were right an' all. The day y'r Grandad were took with a stro'ok a-driving the train, she knew 'aforehand, yer see.'

Superstition ruled our family. Mother got in a state when there was a hole in the loaf, or a picture fell off the wall for no good reason. Perhaps that was why she never stopped eating, to give herself the strength to face things. When it wasn't food, it was sweets. Life was one long meal. 'Run an' git me a quarter a' them butter mixtures. An' I'll 'ave a bar a' milk chocolate an' all. Tell Mrs Gayes I'll settle up Friday. Git a move on, bookworm!' she bawled at me.

Mrs Gayes who kept the corner shop was a wispy little woman with eyes looking in different directions. When I asked her for a tin of Rowntree's cocoa, she gave me a tin of apricots standing beside it. She coughed and snuffled with a permanent cold. The gas jet spluttered over the sweets laid out in boxes, making them look wet and shiny, as though someone had been sucking them.

'She shuun't be servin' in that shop with 'er catarrh,' Mum laid the law down as she munched her chocolate, 'but I'm not goin' ter report 'er 'cause she put things on the slate for me.' By this time Mother had begun to blow up like a balloon. I watched her uneasily. I tried to please her. Mum had a strong feeling no one liked her. Most of all Father. 'Snake,' she called him one night, as he drank his cocoa. She stopped ironing and glared at him.

''Oo're yew callin' a snake?' Father protested.

'It's what y'are.' She spat on the iron, making it hiss.

'Whatever are yew mobbin' about now? Always finding fault, in't yer?'

Although he said this under his breath she heard it and flew at him. 'Findin' fault!' she roared, her face hectic. 'I're got good reason, in't I? Wot life 'ave I ever 'ad since I married yew? Yew sucked me in all right. Lumbered me wi' two kids right quick.'

'Yew wanted kids,' Father said, easing his finger round the collar of his shirt.

'I wanted 'em, did I?', she seethed. 'It were yew, not me. I were all right as I was. All I wanted were ter git away from me Mother. I wun't a-married yew, if I'd 'ave 'ad a proper 'oom.' Tears gushed as she slammed the iron down, crushing his shirt underneath it.

'I'm orf out a' this,' Dad searched for his jacket, which she had hidden. 'Where's my jacket?'

'Yer not 'avin' it!' There was a crash and the sound of wood splintering, as Dad tried to bolt out of the back door. She slammed it quick, trapping him half-way. She pushed with all her strength to close the door. Father lurched forward and she pitched down. He was on top of her in a second, pinning her down. We watched sick with terror as Father clamped both hands round her throat, eyes glazed, driven out of his senses. A gurgle came out of her like a tap being turned off, she couldn't speak.

We tugged at his hands shouting: 'Dad, let go, let go!' But his fingers were made of iron, they wouldn't uncoil from Mother's throat. She was on her last gasp, her face purple.

All at once, he came to himself, shook his head twice and let go. He was like someone coming out of a nightmare. Mother got to her feet and staggered towards the couch, her neck like fire, covered in red marks. Father was still on his knees looking dazed.

'Git yew orf ter bed, yew two,' she croaked. Her voice had gone so feeble we could hardly understand her.

It was over. Perhaps we had saved her life that night. But she didn't change. She still went on trying to get her own way. Gradually Father gave in more and more and the rows lessened. He began to take a back seat in our lives.

However much Mum played up, Dad never wanted her to go. But the rows wore him out whereas she thrived on them.

'Yew want ter dip that lettuce in vinegar and sprinkle it wi' sugar, Gal Audrey.' Dad handed me a big curly one out of his garden. That was Dad's salad dressing. He chewed his food methodically, his lips closed. I watched his Adam's apple jumping up and down. Mum munched and talked all the time, so you could see what she was eating.

'I don't 'old wi' lettuces,' she snapped, 'my father said they was full a' loddamin.'

'Loddamin,' Dad scratched his head, 'there in't no loddamin in lettuces, so far as I know on.'

Mum looked peevish. 'You *will* contradict me, won't yer.'

'I unly says what I thinks. I'm entitled ter do that,' Dad bristled. In his old grey jacket he sat at the table looking tired. His eyes were grey as well, soft and shy. Above them, his forehead rose up like a beacon. Dad's forehead was outstanding. It showed intelligence, much as he tried to hide it from Mum. I knew he had a brain and I loved brains.

'Twist everything I say. Blummin' cunnin', thaa's what y'are.' Mum accused Dad of having secrets he was keeping to himself. Quiet people were always cunning, so she claimed.

'What do you mean?' Dad asked, looking shocked. I could see black rings round the pupils of his eyes like an eagle. Then his lids came down and he jiffled about in embarrassment. He wasn't guilty, but she made him *feel* guilty, the way she did us.

'What do you mean?' he asked again, shifting nervously.

Our family were always asking each other what they meant. But they never seemed to give a proper answer. They all talked a lot, but they didn't really make themselves clear to each other. Yet I knew what Dad wanted to say before he spoke. I could tell by how he looked.

'Yew know very well what I mean,' Mum snorted. I watched them both, knowing what would happen next. He would walk out to avoid a row. He scraped his chair, coughed and went up the garden.

'D'ye hear!' she barked, putting her red face out of the kitchen window. Father tried not to, as he stirred the bowl of chicken-feed in the shed.

'Can't yew answer me?' she bawled. ''Ave I got ter come out there ter yew?' He flew out in a panic, lumps of meal dropping off the spoon. A wet towel on the line flapped in his face.

'I never 'eard yew call. Wot d'ye want?'

I sat on my swing feeling uneasy. Mum had just washed my hair in camomile lotion, still hoping to lighten it from dark brown to gold. My scalp was sore where she'd jabbed at it with her sharp fingers. I wished my brother would come home, in case there was another fight and Dad was quelled forever. I couldn't contemplate that. Dad stood between me and Mum. If he went, I would be finished.

My brother free-wheeled through the gate, whipping off his

skull-cap. The torn bit in the front stuck up on his head like a little horn.

'Waa's up?' he asked. He got off and squeezed his front tyre critically.

'Row,' I said. His face went long and serious.

'Tea ready yet?' he demanded, changing the subject.

'Bloaters,' I said. 'But I'm not eatin' 'em.'

'Daft ha'porth,' he said, 'yew never eat nothin', thaa's why yer always gettin' things wrong with yer.'

'Don't care,' I shouted. Then, without meaning to, I burst into tears.

'Yer grizzling to git sympathy!' he said, pushing past.

Dad and Mum shouted at each other in the kitchen. Mum forgot the frying pan. It caught fire and the fish was burnt up. She really let herself go, flinging herself into a chair, sobbing into her apron, her chest heaving up and down; while the three of us watched.

Baffled, Dad quietly disappeared. After a few minutes he came back holding his hand out. On his palm sat four speckled eggs. They were new laid with little bits of fluff sticking to them.

'Eggs,' he said with pride, 'that little ole hen jus' laid 'em. There's one each.'

'Whopping big ones too,' Dennis said, brightening up.

Mother sprang forward and plucked the eggs out of Dad's fist. Quick as a flash she smashed them, one by one, on the breeze blocks. For one moment I thought Dad would go for her. He lunged forward, but she side-stepped and he hurtled past and fell in the yellow slime. His grey flannels were covered in egg. The folly of it brought him back to reality. He had no other trousers to go to work in.

'Yew c'n git yer own teas,' Mum shouted over her shoulder. 'I'm orf an' I shan't be back.' She heaved on her old brown coat with the moth-eaten fur collar, her green off-the-face hat was stuck on the back of her head.

' 'Strewth!' Dad muttered. The house had gone very quiet. He looked expectantly at us, as though waiting for us to say something. But we were silent. So he went up the garden again and we trailed behind him into the shed.

Our shed was full of mice. They gorged on the bags of maize for the chickens. That was why we had Minnie, but she hardly touched the mice. Instead she hid in a corner near the meat-safe and nabbed the Sunday brisket. Mum had put a stop to it by moving the safe into the pantry and Minnie was famished. I was sitting on my swing when I saw her jump high in the air and come down on top of a mouse. I ran to the rescue and forced her to part with it. She snarled, her mouth open wide like the lion on MGM pictures.

'Naughty Minnie,' I scolded. Her eyes narrowed with hatred. I examined the mouse. It had gone all flat. Its eyes were closed, yet its heart was thumping against my palm. I made a warm bed for it out of my fleecy-lined knickers and put drops of milk on its face. It didn't move. I held it gently, as I swung. It was gone. I would have to dig a grave for it. Tears squeezed out of my eyes.

Minnie crept forward on her haunches. 'Murderer!' I shouted. 'You've killed somebody, look!' To shame her, I held out the corpse. Instantly, the mouse revived, scuttled up my arm and down my back, straight into the shed. Minnie pounced again, but landed on thin air. I laughed, glad I wouldn't have to dig a grave after all.

But graves had to be dug in our garden sometimes. My dog Chum had been run over by the baker's van. He lay in the gutter and jerked twice, then he was dead. I mourned him a long while. Then my duck fell into the jaws of next door's new puppy. He had sharp teeth and feathers flew everywhere. I wrote poems to the deceased and sealed them up in boxes. There they lay till judgment day. Mum said I was mur-hearted, she didn't get upset the way I did.

The only death that had affected Mum was the budgie. Mum had a way with budgies. She could make them talk. She bullied them night and day till they answered her back. Mum wouldn't let anything beat her. The budgie put his head on one side and said: 'Pretty boy, pretty boy.' When Dad came home, he squawked out: ''Allo Charlie boy.' Then we'd gone away on holiday and left him with Mrs Harford next door. While we were away, Joey lost the power of speech.

'That damn budgie can't talk no more,' Mum said bitterly. ''E's gone an' reverted to a bird.'

Dad couldn't stop laughing. Some of the things Mum said really tickled him. He rocked from side to side, his face screwed up, laughing silently. She said he was 'goldering'. She never joined in. She couldn't understand why what she had said was funny. The only thing that really made her laugh were babies. Mum loved babies. She stared into their little creased-up faces and nodded and jabbered, as though they could understand everything she said. Mum preferred things she could boss. If they had a will of their own, she wasn't interested. She put them down quickly.

All this went through my mind as I swung faster and faster, till I got a tickly feeling in my belly. I put my head back and closed my eyes and the whole world went round and round. I was up in the sky in an aeroplane. I sang softly to myself: '*Amy, wonderful Amy, I'm proud of the way you flew.*' It was Mum's favourite song.

Perhaps she was back. I went in to look for her. But she wasn't there. I switched on the light and saw the photograph on the living-room wall of a baby with dark corkscrew curls. I wondered if that baby had made Mum laugh. I knew I wasn't what Mum wanted; she often said so. I wandered round the house feeling scared in case she'd gone for good. Then I noticed her handbag in the middle of the table. It had a broken handle and wouldn't close properly; the leather had gone rotten and it was torn down the side. I picked it up and hugged it against my chest. I knew she would come back. She never went anywhere without that bag.

Dad came in and washed his hands, then sat down with his newspaper. Dennis was reading Pip, Squeak and Wilfred. Just then the door burst open and Mum waltzed in. We all gazed at her. She was in a good mood. Dad put a match to the fire and we all perked up. Mum dumped a big parcel of chips on the table.

'I met y'r Auntie Beattie,' she said, 'we went in the fish shop an' y'r Uncle Sid was there, so 'e treated us at the Cherry Tree.' She winked at me and glanced slyly at Dad. But for once he wasn't jealous.

11
Down the Backwater

'Butt'er!' Mother burst out. 'I never knew what butt'er was till I married y'r Father.' She paused to finish chewing, her cheeks puffed out. She'd wedged her mouth so full she could hardly speak. Yet she managed to give the word all the savour it deserved. When she said 'butt'er' you could taste it. You could see glistening yellow slabs of it waiting to be thickly spread. 'We never 'ad unly marge in our 'ouse, when I were young. Once yew gits the taste a' best butter, yew never want nothin' else.'

Mum loved butter; not just on bread, but lumps of it gouged out with a knife. She licked it off the blade and rolled it round her tongue. I could hear her smacking her lips as she studied the half-pound packet in front of her with worshipping eyes.

To Mother, every meal was a feast. She gorged herself. Plump she was and swelling like a loaf in the oven. She even had a yeasty smell.

I watched her lacing herself into her stays, which were more like a suit of armour. 'Yew can see I in't got no stummick in my "Little X",' she gasped, thumping her belly. It sounded hollow and crackled like stiff paper.

While Mother ate, I starved myself and had no appetite. I was sickly and sent home regularly with notes from school.

Dear Mrs Emms
Audrey looks washed-out. I wonder whether she is really well enough to come to school. Could you take her to the doctor?
Yours etc.,
Gwendoline Olorenshaw

'What a neck she's got, that ole frump!' Mum snapped. She knew my headmistress took an interest in me and she resented it. An old maid with eyeglasses and hair in a bun had a cheek to write her letters!

But Mum had to admit I *was* peaky. 'Gal Audrey,' she barked, 'yer what I call a pingler. You don't never want nothin' to eat. I don't know why I'm bothered to cook all this bootiful food fer you. I detest cookin' an' I detest waitin' on other people, as it is.'

She stalked into the kitchen, swearing under her breath. Everything was upside down, the way it always was. All the things in the larder joined forces against Mother the minute she got in amongst them. They either fell on the floor and got trodden into the coconut matting, or they hid away from her in corners and couldn't be found. As soon as she tackled the washing-up, the sink blocked itself up and the soap fell into the spuds when she drained them. The spoons all disappeared and whenever she opened the door of her meat-safe the flies jumped out at her. ''Owever did them sods git in therè?' she snorted, as they circled round the naked bulb. She glared at the meat. It was crawling and writhing.

'Strike a light!' she fumed. 'That meat's tainted! It'll 'ave ter be soaked in vinegar now, dew that'll be on its last legs. Better git some air in 'ere.' She flew at the kitchen window and smashed it open. The stained yellow curtains blew in the breeze and knocked down the piles of stuff on the window-sill; sticks of celery, bunches of watercress and sliced beetroot all fell down into the drain.

'Now thaa's y'r Father agin, in't it?' she wailed, ''e would put that lot up there. Thaa's the sort a' tricks 'e gits up to, just ter rile me up.'

'All you do is crab,' Dad muttered. He always got the blame.

Mother trailed outside in her pink overall, hair dangling in her eyes. She bent down and fished the vegetables out of the drain, then dashed them up and down in her chipped enamel bowl and flung them on the plates in front of us, showering us with water. Her temper was up, my brother and I cringed and glanced anxiously at Dad. He would have to answer to God for the trouble he had caused. But he took it in good part and helped himself to the salad. He was entitled to; he'd grown it. He cut off a piece of cheese which was enough to satisfy a small mouse. Like me, he was not a good eater. Mum calmed down and made herself comfortable, talking and eating all at once; slurping her tea.

'It want a bit more milk in this,' she sniffed, grabbing the bottle. 'Milk they calls it, more like water! Look at the colour on it.'

That was how Mum spoke, or rather, how the words burst out of her. She had a gift for the dramatic, especially when it came to food. She would get hold of a word and bandy it about, turn it inside out and make it work for her until it gave up its true meaning.

'Meat,' she snorted, 'don't talk ter me about meat! It don't do ter talk about it. I got a bit a' brisket the other day, I swear it were more 'n a 'undred year old. Yew cuu'n't even git yer teeth into it. It were all black an' all.'

She didn't mention that she'd kept it for five days in her meat-safe, then soaked it in vinegar to kill the reek of decomposition before she baked it.

I watched her, biting my nails with resentment, trying to understand. Understand Mother! Some hopes. Some days I got on with her, others I couldn't do anything right. She was unpredictable, tempestuous and suspicious. But I envied her ready tongue. Whatever she said sounded forceful and full of meaning.

When she said 'soot' it sounded black and dense, 'washing' on her lips conveyed the feeling of hard work. Or the word 'crafty' made you see someone with beady eyes. 'Bullick' produced an image of a great horned beast. It was the way she used her Norfolk speech; she made it pictorial.

It was sunny and warm when we got up one Sunday morning. The meat was definitely off. This time, Mum threw it straight in the bin. It was a good excuse to get out of cooking Sunday lunch.

'Come on, you lot,' she bawled, 'let's take some bread an' butter out to Whitlingham. We'll 'ave a day in the open air. I'm fed up wi' the sight a' this damn 'ouse. Run an' ask the Plunketts ter come with us, Gal Audrey.'

Mrs Plunkett was Mum's best friend of the moment. She was a stout ungainly woman with a smallish head and short black hair. She had light brown eyes and no eyelashes and a hoarse monotonous voice. 'Mum says, would you like to come to Whitlingham with us?' I said, when she finally opened her door. I stood outside, twisting my feet about. Mrs Plunkett always made me worried.

She pondered a long while, scratched her head and said: 'Course, I c'n see yer all riddy ter go, in't yer? Then yer Mum'd 'ave ter wait fer us, wun't she? That'll 'old yew all up, wun't it?'

I couldn't think how to reply, so I went on fidgeting. Their daughter, Rio Rita, who was the same age as me, peered out from behind her Mum. 'I want ter go with 'em,' she whined.

'Shut yew up, Rita. We in't 'ad our breakfas' yit, 'ave we?'

'Don't want none. I want ter go with them. Billy want ter go as well.'

'Oh well, if Billy want ter go, then I better say yiss.' Mrs Plunkett worshipped her boy Billy. She put her hefty arm round his skinny shoulders. 'Let's git yew dressed then, my pet.' He was eleven and she waited on him hand and foot.

'I'll tell Mum yer comin'.' I ran home to find Mum in her V-necked grey grosgrain with her straw hat tied under her chin. It had a big dent in the side, where someone had sat on it accidentally.

'Mum, what've you got them goloshes on for? It's a nice day. 'Tisn't wet.'

'These'll dew fer sploddin' about down the backwater with.'

Excited, we set off for Whitlingham river. It was a route march, with the men charging on in front and the women trying to keep up. The fresh air made us sing, as we headed for Trowse, the first village outside the city walls.

> *'You are my lucky star,*
> *I saw you from afar,*
> *And I was star-struck . . .'*

Mum was off key, but we were pleased when she joined in.

'See the light'ouse?' Dad teased, pointing to the flour mills. It was an old joke. People said the North Sea had flooded once as far as Trowse, so they had built a lighthouse, although it was twenty miles inland.

Past Trowse station, with the little fringes of woodwork outside the ticket office, on over the bridge we trudged. Once we turned into Whitlingham Lane it was all country for miles around, flat and marshy, with rabbits popping out and water rats scuttling away from our feet. Mum was forging ahead now. 'Come on, yew lot, I'm gittin' damn 'ungry.'

Dad had brought a rubber sheet for us to sit on. 'Put that down over here, Charlie, near the river, away from that cowshit.'

She flung herself down, giggling and showing her legs. 'Come on Fred, yew sit next ter me.' Fred Plunkett had been keeping his eye on Mum all the way there, but so had Dad and Fred was no fool. Dad's colour had come up.

'Strike a light, Gal Gladys,' he gulped, smoothing down his greasy hair, 'your Charlie'll want ter sit next ter yew.' He made way for Dad. Then we all moved up to let Mrs Plunkett sit down. 'Come yew on, Winnie.' Her husband helped to lower her down. He winked at Mum behind his wife's back.

'Now, you kids,' Mum barked, 'jam, or bread an' sugar?' She'd cut the bread thick and put butter on hers and marge on ours. Still, it tasted all right and even tap-water tasted better out of a lemonade bottle. There were Mother's short cakes too, stained with the blood of a few currants.

'Yew'll 'ave one a' my short cakes, Fred,' she smiled at him as she held out a brown paper bag shiny with grease.

'I wouldn't mind one a' yore dumplin's, Gladys,' Fred whispered.

'Cheeky devil,' Mother beamed. Father glared at the opposite bank of the river where a bird with a long beak was darting back and forth.

'Why, thaa's a kingfisher, Gal Audrey, look at that!'

'Oh Dad,' I breathed, 'in't it lovely!'

The long calm stretch of water looked inviting. I wiped the jam off my lips with the back of my hand and pulled my costume out from under the bread and butter packet.

'Yer never goin' inter that water, Gal Audrey,' Mother snapped. 'Yer'll git yore death.'

Father stuck up for me. 'It's not that cold, Gladys.'

'Keep your nose out. 'Oo ask yew?'

By the time the row was under way I had changed and was wading out into the river. I hung on to a willow branch and moved gingerly along in the mud at the bottom. It gave way all at once and I pitched down. I opened my mouth to shout and the water rushed in. I sank like a stone. A second later, I came up and caught a glimpse of the family as I went down again. They hadn't noticed me. They were still arguing while I was drowning. I struggled among the weeds, trying to find a hand-hold. A voice was hissing in my ears. It was Uncle Donald. I couldn't understand what he was doing at the bottom of the river.

'If yew dare ter tell yore Mother anything about this, I'll drown yer in Thorpe River.' It was coming true, though I had never told Mum what he'd forced me to do. My ears roared, my eyes burned, there was no sensation in my legs at all. I was getting weaker. My arms flailed and I banged against a solid object; a rubber tyre was floating past. I caught hold of it and hung on. Daylight blinded me as I surfaced again. I kicked out and drifted in towards the bank. I could hardly believe I had been saved after all.

I hauled myself up the bank, clinging to roots and twigs. My tongue felt like a piece of wood and I was coughing up bits of bright green stuff. Crawling on all fours out of the mud, I peered round. They hadn't even missed me. I shook the water off my long hair.

'Hold yew 'ard, young Audrey,' an angry voice snorted, 'whatever dew yew think you're doin', throwin' water all over me?'

I shrank back from the massive body lying prone beside me on the grass. Mrs Plunkett's beady eyes glared into mine. She was covered in grease and had been sunbathing.

'Sorry, Mrs Plunkett,' I spluttered, and crawled back into the river without another word. I started practising the strokes that Dad had taught me down at the baths. Whatever happened, I would learn to swim now. I wasn't going to drown like that again.

'If you pull a face like that, I'll smack your chops.' Mum meant what she said, but I couldn't help scowling. I didn't want to go to Yarmouth. It was spitting with rain and I knew where we'd end up: at the Amusement Arcade. Mum had the gambler's itch, but to my brother and me it was a lot of squit. Besides, we'd blued our pocket money.

'Do you put them other shoes on now,' Mum snapped. 'I've blanco'ed them for yer.' They were still wet and besides that, they were flat. I was ten and fancied a pair of courts, like Auntie Renee was wearing.

'Crikey, Boy Dennis,' Mum shrieked at my brother, 'yer not in that damn closet agin, are yer? Whatever are yew a-doing in there?'

Just then I heard the chain and my brother came out, doing his buttons up. 'I'll 'ave ter dew 'alf 'ere and 'alf when I gits on the train,' he grumbled.

'Obstinate!' Mum rapped out. 'Yew want some med'cine down a' yew.' It was all up with Dennis, I thought. Still, he'd brought it on himself. He knew what Mum was like, the same as I did; a stickler for her own way.

Auntie Renee was carrying a bottle of brown stuff with her. She took the cork out and handed it round, giggling; 'Liquorice wine,' she said, 'you can't beat it.'

Mum sniffed at it and pushed it away. ''Strewth,' she snorted, 'wherever did yew git that? Out a' the closet?' Mother stared suspiciously at her sister. 'Yew've got a rare colour.' She looked in the glass again. 'What dew I look like?'

'Not ser bad as yesterday,' was the honest reply. Renee was always straightforward. She was the only one in the family Mother could trust. She looked nice in her mustard cardigan. It was long, like the one Greta Garbo had worn in *Queen Christina*. I couldn't wait to be like Auntie; she had a bust and proper hips. I drew my waist in tight with Mum's leather belt, to see if my hips stood out like Auntie's. I was looking forward to being fourteen one day and having the swagger coat Mum had promised me.

'All on board,' the guard shouted, glaring at us. My brother went down on his hands and knees as we tore through the barrier. Mum hadn't paid for him, but he wasn't noticed in the rush. The platform was black and greasy with drizzle. It was disheartening for our day out. I recognised the peculiar tang of the wet cinders between the lines. It reminded me of grandfather, who was an engine driver and sometimes took us all out free, because we were family.

The whistle blasted out and the engine gave a whoop of delight. Gathering speed, it thundered out of Thorpe Station. It slowed down again after about two miles and ground to a halt, wheezing, panting, brakes screeching. A smell of sulphur, like washing-day, wafted up. I let down the window on the leather strap and hung out. 'Cow on the line,' I shouted, forgetting I was supposed to be Jean Harlow in *Hell's Angels* in a tight-fitting flying suit.

Mother was trying to get herself settled down. Carriages were small and cramped in those days, because people weren't as big then. 'Look at them seats,' she burst out, 'aren't they pewtrid. Talk about catching diseases.' She spread a newspaper over them. I daren't laugh, but her face tickled me. She really thought we'd all go down with typhoid.

'Come yew in an' sit yew down, Gal Audrey,' Mum yelled, 'dew someone else'll take your seat.' She hadn't noticed we were the only ones on the train. The newspaper crackled underneath me. I pulled it out and read: 'Herr Hitler Rounds Up the Jews'.

Auntie read it out over my shoulder. ''Oo is this Her' Titler?' she asked, puzzled.

Mother roared, her shoulders shaking, 'Her' Hitler, not Her' Titler! Trust yew ter git it right, yew barmy ha'porth!'

Auntie took it in good part. She smiled proudly, her round face lighting up. She had a reputation in the family for being a bit daft. 'Well, I'm just askin', in't I? 'Oo is 'e?'

''E in't a much'er, thaa's fer sure. I reckin 'e want a good punch in the snout.'

'An wot dew it mean about the Jews? 'Oo is the Jews?' Auntie could be stubborn, when she wanted to find out something. She never took sides though, because she didn't know exactly which side she was on.

'I'm sure I couldn't say,' said Mum, losing interest. 'There in't none round 'ere, not that I know on.' The train rocked, lulling her into a trance. She stared at the advertisements for Dolly Blue Bags and Force Wheatflakes, which had a man leaping over the moon. She gradually dropped off. A minute later she opened her eyes and sat bolt upright. 'Where's that Boy Denny gone to?' She'd just noticed he was missing, and the train had stopped.

Auntie signalled with her eyes towards the toilet. ''E's in there,' she whispered, 'they c'n 'ave yew fer that, y'know. We aren't even moving.'

Mum flew at the toilet door. 'Come out a' there, yew little snot.' She nearly had the door off.

'Leave off,' my brother grumbled, safe and sound inside, 'I're nearly finished.'

'Git out a' there this minute!'

I was giggling. The squabble was amusing, so long as it wasn't me Mum had her knife into. As soon as Dennis came out, she dragged him bodily into the compartment and wrenched his jacket off. 'An' don't mess that new coat up, dew I'll pay you.' He ground his teeth, while I took the laugh.

'Pardon us, ladies, can we get past please?' The cheeky voice took us by surprise. Two men had got on the train between stations.

Mum's expression changed. I never saw anyone's face alter so quickly as Mum's when she wanted to. 'Oh certainly,' she cooed, making up to them straightaway. They pushed past, stared at Auntie and plonked themselves down beside her. They both looked shifty, but full of bounce. Nothing like Dad, who was reserved and hadn't much to say for himself. But at least you knew where you were with Dad. I couldn't say the same about these two.

'Gaddin' about, yew two girls?' one said, taking half a Woodbine from behind his ear and striking a match on his shoe. He edged closer to Auntie in her white piqué skirt. I saw her give him the glad eye quite distinctly. I couldn't understand why. He was nothing like Ronald Colman, her favourite.

'Want a sweet, my beauty?' he handed me a chocolate drop. He was treating me like a child. He didn't realise I was Jean Harlow.

'Give us a bit,' my brother said. I bit half and gave it to him, but he handed it back. 'That taste funny,' he said, spitting.

I watched the two men. Neither had collars on, nor did they look too clean. But I could see they knew their way about; they had such sharp eyes. One of them noticed I was sitting on the *Sunday Pictorial*. He spotted a blonde in a bathing costume.

'C'n I 'ave a look at your paper, ole dear?' I dragged it out and gave it to him, all crumpled and warm. The seat was prickly now, so I stood in the corridor. My brother followed me. The meadows were drenched and full of steaming cows. The scenery was monotonous, just one tree after another. I wished our train was like the one in *The Great Ziegfeld*, where people talked foreign and had drinks with cherries in them.

Mum had started a conversation, 'D'ye come from Norwich, then?' she asked, pretending it didn't really interest her.

'No, Swaffham,' they said, drumming their feet and imitating the tango.

'Wot're yew doin' round 'ere, then? Lookin' fer a job, is that it?' Auntie Renee sounded suspicious.

'Job? Oh no, not likely. We're goin' to enlist.'

'Lot a' fules,' Mum snorted, forgetting herself. She had two brothers in the regulars, who couldn't wait to get out.

'What, in the Royal Norficks?' Auntie asked.

'Yep, that's it, the Norficks.' They went on drumming.

Auntie looked down on soldiers. Most people did. Anyone who couldn't get a job went and joined up. All the throw-outs.

'Three square meals and a bob a day,' they grinned, ''tin't ser bad.'

'Yer welcome,' Mum said.

I watched the scenery again. The weather had cleared up and the fields were full of bluebells. I could almost touch them from the train window. I was daydreaming about Tony, who was older than me and had a racer. I saw us together on a tandem, cycling into the distance. Just then I heard a scream that ended up in a giggle. To my surprise the blinds of our compartment had been pulled down and a scuffle was going on inside. Before my brother could dive in, I grabbed his arm. 'Hold yew hard,' I hissed.

'What're yew gone barmy?' he shouted, fighting to get away.

'If yew let 'em alone in there,' I whispered, 'they might give us something.'

'Such as?' he stopped struggling.

'A ha'penny, or even a penny,' I suggested, rolling my eyes. I understood his mentality. He was saving up to buy a gun.

'Yer got a neck,' he spluttered, straightening his pullover, so the hole underneath the arm didn't show. 'Yew tore that,' he accused, 'I'm tellin' Mum.'

Just then, one of the blinds flew up. There sat Mum with her big knees all bare. Her skirt was up and she was smoking a cigarette as well. I watched her spellbound. Auntie was sitting on the freckled one's lap. I always thought she was bashful, but her cardigan was off and he was fondling her shoulder. It reminded me of that story in *Secrets* magazine called 'Depths of Depravity'. But Mum was all smiles for once, so she must be enjoying it. Yet she always said men were no good.

They saw me staring at them. One of the men pointed at me and said: 'You don't look old enough to have a girl that size.' I felt ashamed and went back to being ten again. His Adam's apple jumped up and down as he spoke, reminding me of Dad. But his hair started lower down on his forehead and his chin was hairy as well. That was why he looked so scruffy.

'Oh no, the children don't belong to me, honest,' Mum laughed wildly in his direction. 'They belongs ter me sister.' The lies came out without any hesitation. She had it pat. Dennis and I looked at each other in amazement.

'I thought you said *she* was your sister, and she told us she hadn't got any kids.' He indicated Auntie with the point of his chin, but she didn't notice. She was lying back on the other man's shoulder, her eyes glazed and sleepy. Her dress had come undone and the bottle of liquorice wine was rolling about empty on the floor.

'Oh no, not *that* sister,' Mum blushed, 'we're several in family. I're got three more at home, older than me.' She had put on her swanky voice now.

'How do she make that out?' My brother prodded me in the shoulder with his sharp finger.

'She don't mean it,' I explained, 'look, she's half drunk.' But I was dumbfounded. What was Mum's game?

They rolled the blind down and shut us out again. The train shuddered, sighed and came to a stop. 'Brundall Halt.' I read out the name to my brother. He couldn't read yet; he was a dunce.

'Yew rotter,' he turned on me in a fury, 'you said they was goin' to give us some money, din't yew!'

'Just go in and say you want a Snofruit and see what they say.'

'I'm not goin' in there,' he hissed, 'I can't hear nothin' and I can't see nothin'; how do I know what they're doin' of?'

'You're yellow,' I said, and pushed him away from me.

'It's all very well for you, you're a girl.'

The door slid back and the bloke who'd been with Auntie sidled out, then shut it again quickly. It was dark inside. He ignored us altogether and made for the toilet. Without his jacket with the padded shoulders he looked puny. We heard him singing: '*Oh, we ain't got a barrel of money, maybe we're ragged and funny.*' Then he pulled the chain and came out, smoothing down his hair, which was all over the place.

The train got up steam and went flat out the rest of the way.

'Yarmouth Vauxhall, we're here,' I shouted. I stepped back as Mum came out of the compartment, arm in arm with Auntie. They both looked flushed and pleased with themselves.

'Wot d'ye think a' that?' Mum pushed her arm under my

nose. On her wrist was a chromium-plated watch. 'It's a keepsake,' she said.

I put my ear to it. 'It don't go,' I said.

'That don't matter. It's a lovely watch just the same.'

'Coo, Mum,' I said enviously, 'it don't 'alf look smart.'

'There in't no need to tell y'r Father,' she said, 'jus' say I found it on the train.' I nodded with a serious face. No one had a wristwatch in our family.

The two blokes were lying down on the seats with the blinds drawn. 'We're 'avin' a kip,' they called out. 'Mind what yer up to, yew two mawthers. See yew up the Lido.' I knew that meant something smutty.

Mum didn't answer them, but she was in a good mood just the same. The engine let off steam with a great blast as we strolled along the platform. Mum made straight for the cockle stall on Yarmouth market. She had her sleeves pulled up, so you could see the watch. We had cockles, mussels and whelks and finished up with a dish of hot pease pudding.

That was one of the best days we ever had at Yarmouth. The rain had stopped and we sang 'Swanee River' all the way home. We never told Father either. Thinking it over in bed that night, before I went to sleep, I realised something I didn't know before. There was no doubt about it – Mum had 'It'. To think I'd never even noticed it before.

I stared at myself in Mum's looking-glass. By adjusting the panels I could see both sides. I was sure there was a lump on my chest. I ripped off my school blouse and liberty bodice to get a better view. Yes, there it was, underneath my nipple, like a tiny bud. I touched it gingerly. It was hard and hot. It must be proud flesh. I'd got another boil coming up.

Remembering what I'd gone through with the last one made me groan. A big lump had come up on my thigh. 'Hot fomentations,' Mum had snapped. Her eyes, hard as steel, frightened me. 'Gal Audrey's got a "push" on 'er leg an' it's got ter be squeezed out.' Her fingers clamped round my leg like a vice; the pain was unbearable, my leg ached and throbbed.

'Keep still, will you, and stop that grizzling. I got to get the core out, dew the pus'll go all over yew an' yew'll blow up like a balloon. There's no tellin' where you'll end up.'

She slapped a scalding flannel on the boil and held it there with all her strength, clouds of steam rising up. I shrieked.

'Steady on,' Dad muttered, 'dew yew'll end up scalding the gal.'

'Mind y'r own business. Who ask yew to put your snout in? Yew git on wi' your jobs and I'll git on wi' mine.'

'Yew want to 'ave a bit a' sympathy,' Dad said.

'Sympathy!' she screamed. 'Thaa's something you know nothin' about.' Dad put his cap on and went off down the garden, his face flushed.

All this went through my mind as I stared in the glass. Then I shoved my head quickly through the neck of my blouse, Mum was coming upstairs. She mustn't know. I would keep it to myself, even if this time it meant hospital. Every day the lump got a bit bigger and hurt even more, especially in bed. I couldn't bear to touch it. I was glad the school holidays had started, so I wouldn't have to lean over my desk. That made it worse.

One Saturday morning Mum shouted: 'Come on 'ere, Gal Audrey, we're all goin' ter Yarmouth fer the day. I'm no home-bird in weather like this, I like ter git on the beach. Yew can 'ave that frock on wot I bought at the Co-op. Now look slippy.'

What about the bump, I thought? She'll see it, if I'm not careful. I kept my vest on, but she spotted it straightaway. 'Whatever 'ave yew got that vest on for, on a day like this? It look real on-sightly.' I trailed upstairs and took it off. Instead, I put on my cardigan and buttoned it up.

'Whatever are yew playin' at, my lady,' Mum flew at me, 'on a sweatin' 'ot day you've got to 'ave a great wool coat on? You're askin' fer a clout, in't yew?' Then she roared at Father, 'That Gal Audrey's tryin' ter rear me up. I're got the grub ter git riddy, your shirt ter iron an' Boy Denny want buttons on 'is flies. I'm that dis'eartened.'

Dad switched on the wireless to drown her out. 'Scattered sunshine, temperatures reaching sixty-five degrees, falling sharply towards evening . . .'. The weather forecast gave me an idea. 'Mum, can I put my costume on underneath, so I don't have to change on the beach?'

She glared at me. 'Dew wot yew like. I'm finished.' Then she yelled at Dad, who'd gone down the garden: 'D'ye 'ear! Git me some a' that rew'bub, I want ter make a tart fer afters.'

Father laid the rhubarb sticks on the kitchen table, still red, raw and bleeding, where he had cut them. Just then a caterpillar inched out, very perky, arching its back and sitting up. It was all soft and velvety, with tiny horns going in and out like telescopes. I put my finger out to stroke it. With one swipe the bread knife came down and sliced it in two. It lay among the big crumpled leaves oozing sticky stuff out of its body.

'Oh Mum! You've killed it!' I squealed.

'Certainly I 'ave, yew dunno what diseases that thing 'ave got.'

'But it wasn't doing any harm,' I said. But she didn't care for nothing, nor nobody. She often said it.

Mum put on her crêpe de Chine two-piece. She'd made it from a Weldon's pattern called 'A dear little frock for the dull days'. But as soon as we got on the beach the wind blew it over her head. Dad got her a deck-chair and she sank down gasping, with her skirt riding up to her waist. 'This blasted dress 'as got a tizzy on it! We'd better git somewhere more sheltered.' She waltzed off before we could catch up. Dad had his new trilby on and a pair of grey flannels with twenty-one-inch bottoms. They flapped in the breeze, exposing his boots.

'Whyever din't yew put y'r shoes on, 'stead a' them bo-ats. They don't look too cracky ter come down the seaside in. Yer got some funny ideas.'

'I never thought on it,' Dad mumbled, 'still, I c'n git them polished up a bit. There's a bootblack over there.' He pointed to a dark-skinned man with a monkey in a red jacket tied up to a rope beside him. Both of them had a brooding look as they waited patiently for customers, surrounded by brushes and polish tins.

'That yew wun't. The sun'll go in while we're waitin'.' Mum barked.

The other families strolled past in their best clothes, all the women in print frocks, showing white fleshy arms. Then a group of gypsies in gaudy skirts and headscarves, cradling their babies, throwing their heads back as they laughed.

Mum stopped at the weighing-machine, a wooden contraption with a chair hanging on an iron chain, with weights on each side. 'Give 'em a penny,' she snapped at Dad. When Mum sat on it the chair sagged and hit the concrete. I thought she must have broken it altogether. She jumped off and looked at the dial. 'Twelve stone four! I don't go no twelve stone four,' she roared, slinging the card back at the man. 'Wot d'ye take me for, a' elefrunt? Thaa's a swindle! I'll 'ave my money back.'

'There in't nothin' wrong wi' my machine, missus. I've 'ad it tested by the Corporation. Yer not entitled to anything back.' The man stuck up for himself, but he looked frightened when Mother started shouting.

Dad squared up to him. He was just as scared. 'Look 'ere, borr,' he gulped, 'thaa's my wife yer a-talkin' to.'

'Call y'rself a man!' Mother screeched. Whether she meant Dad or the other man wasn't clear. But suddenly Mum grabbed Dad's arm and flounced off, leaving the crowd gaping. 'Come on, Charlie, ignore 'im. Let's git back ter the beach.'

It had turned chilly by then and the sea was choppy. The deck-chairs flapped and clattered along the wet sand, ending up in the sea. The attendant rushed in after them, getting his trousers wet. We laughed at the sight.

Dad yawned and put his *Passing Show* over his face, with his hat on top. The sand spattered against the paper like rain. Mother glared at him. 'Yew look a rummun. I s'puz yew think yer the Sheik a' Arabee.' Then she started on me. 'Gal Audrey, why don't yew go in the water? Yew always does. What do I bring yew ter the seaside for?'

I didn't answer. But I knew she wouldn't give me any peace. I got behind the deck-chairs and manoeuvred my frock over my head, hiding behind a towel. Mum flicked through her *Home Chat* and munched liquorice allsorts. Then she peered at me over the back of her chair. Before she could say anything, I pelted down the beach in my blue rubber sand-shoes, straight into the sea. The cold water took my breath away. I bobbed about, keeping well under the waves so no one could see me. Every time I struck out with a breast-stroke, I could feel my lump hurting.

My teeth chattered when I came out and my black wool costume stuck to me all over. It was heavy and tight round my chest. As I fled up the beach, two boys started staring at me, then nudged each other and laughed. 'Buffers,' they called out, 'can we feel of your buffers? Come 'ere a minute! You've got lovely ones.'

By the time I got back to our patch at the top, my whole life had changed. Everything was different. It was like getting over a bad illness. At last I knew what the lump really was. I could have kissed Mum and Dad, even my brother. I stopped myself in time.

Mum handed me a towel. 'Git y'rself dry, Gal Audrey, an' don't git cold.' I rubbed my chest hard with the rough towel. Soon I would be just like Carole Lombard and Jean Harlow all rolled in one. Clark Gable would eat out of my hand when I wore that tight black satin top and bare midriff.

It was only two days later when I discovered the lump on the other side. I now had two. The new one wasn't very big to start with, but it caught up in no time. Nothing could stop it.

12
Rude Little Cats!

'Are you the girl who did these disgusting drawings? Speak up! Don't mumble. I intend to get to the truth of this.'

My headmistress waved the grubby scraps of paper in front of me, one by one, passing them on to her deputy. Two black crows in their long gowns, hardly able to hide the excitement in their beaky faces. Miss Guppy took each drawing with a trembling hand, then removed her glasses and goggled at it through a magnifying glass. Crude sketches of big round breasts and huge penises. No words of explanation were needed.

I wanted to laugh; but these two facing me were no laughing matter. I stared at my house shoes, with their square toes and high fronts. 'No,' I whispered, looking up, 'it wasn't me.' One eye glared at me in disbelief, the other at the wall. Miss Trumpington had a cast in that one.

The two women gave each other a meaningful glance before they pounced again. 'But they were found in your purse, weren't they, Audrey Emms! This *is* your purse, isn't it? It's got your label inside it. You can't deny that, can you?'

I couldn't. I had lost it that morning in the playground. Ever since, I'd had an uneasy feeling.

'You are lying, aren't you, Audrey? We know the truth, don't we?' Miss Trumpington's thin colourless lips curled, showing long yellow teeth. Her face had a hectic flush caused by a network of broken veins spreading like a rash across her sagging cheeks. She had a bad heart, it was said, besides a bad temper when crossed. Wisps of grey hair hung over the collar of her gown, but she was nearly bald at the hairline.

I tossed my long black curls and faced up to her. 'No,' I insisted, 'it wasn't me, Miss Trumpington. I'm not telling lies. Someone else drew them.'

Miss Guppy gasped and the head drew herself up, swishing her gown round her. 'How dare you contradict me! Of course you did it. Admit it at once!'

'The truth is Arthur drew them. He put them in an envelope and handed them to me,' I mumbled, my knees shaking. 'I meant to throw them away, but I forgot.' As soon as I had made a clean breast of it, I realised I'd made it much worse. Miss Trumpington sank down as though she was going to cry. Then her hand went to her heart and she leaned heavily on her mahogany desk.

'Dear Lord, I cannot believe my own ears. You mean to say you've been keeping company with a boy! You say *he* drew these disgraceful things?' She sounded almost as terrified as I was. Hovering at the back of my mind was the thought of the girl in the third form who'd been made pregnant by a conductor on the school bus. It had all been hushed up and she'd left in a hurry. But it had been rumoured that the governors had considered closing the whole school down. Only the inconvenience of disposing of five hundred of us had stopped them.

I hung my head again, avoiding the bloodshot eyes boring into me. 'I simply do not believe it. A girl from this school being familiar with boys!' Her voice quavered. The deputy fumbled in the Red Cross cupboard and poured out some brandy into a medicine glass. Her hand was trembling. What would happen to me now? Prison, reform school? My world had crashed. I blinked back tears of fright. I wouldn't let myself cry in front of them. But now they were too busy to notice me. Miss Trumpington was gasping for breath and Miss Guppy was banging her on the back. She'd drunk the brandy too quickly.

Whatever would Mum say, if she knew? But she mustn't find out about this. She was already in a temper over my last report. 'Yew allus seem ter git sich rotten marks f'r condick,' she'd grumbled. 'Waa's the reason fer that?' I couldn't explain to her, but I knew why it was. I couldn't bear all the regimentation at my new school. It was run like an army. I was always in hot water because I couldn't remember the lists of rules I had to keep. House shoes, gym shoes, games shoes to be placed in your shoe bag and hung on the peg. Never go out without your hat and keep your blazer buttons fastened at all times.

'They're too strict, Mum,' I had murmured.

'Too strict, my lady! Yew know nothin'. Yew'd a' bin beaten black an' blew at my school. Yew dunno where yer well orf! Posh school like the Bly'. If it a'n't a' bin fer me yew wun't a' gorn, would yer? Yore Father would a' put yew in a fact'ry like 'im. 'E don't 'old wi' posh schools fer sich as us. It's me wot's done everythin' for yew. I never 'ad yore chances when I were young, did I? I wanted ter see yew make the most on it.' She glared at my report, spelling it out with her finger under the words. 'Condick this term. Very poor. Room for improvement. Audrey must learn that rules are made to be obeyed.'

'And does your mother know you speak to boys?' Miss Trumpington had rallied again after the brandy and her eyes glittered with hate. I hesitated, trying to weigh up the odds in favour of a lie. Truth didn't help me much.

'Yes,' I claimed stoutly.

'Disgusting,' murmured the deputy, dabbing her forehead with a lace handkerchief.

'Oh she does, does she? Well, we'll soon find out!' The head hooted in disbelief. I was trapped. 'This is a very serious matter, Audrey Emms, and I have decided to suspend you from this school until it has been thoroughly investigated. You can go and pack up your things now.'

The big oak door struck my heels. I was a black sinner shut out. I looked up and saw the school motto written in gold: *Be a Blithe Spirit and Spell it with a 'Y'*. I didn't feel very blithe as I shouldered my satchel and dawdled out to the bus stop. What would I tell Mum? I sat on the bus biting my nails.

Mum was just sliding a couple of back rashers into the pan when a letter dropped on the floor next morning. 'It say Mrs G. Emms. That's me, in't it,' she mused, "ooever c'n be writin' ter me?' She hardly ever got letters. She tore it open and scanned it excitedly, then with a face like thunder she held out the bundle of drawings between thumb and forefinger like something infectious. 'Wotever 'ave yew bin up tew, my lady? Yew've disgraced me, 'aven't yew? Wotever is these rude objecks?'

She slumped into a chair and burst into loud sobbing. Now I was shocked. I wanted to comfort her and say it was nothing. I put one hand gingerly round her heaving shoulders, but she jerked away from me. 'Git away from me, yew dirty, rude little cat!' she screamed. 'I doan' know what I're done ter deserve sich a daugh'er. I're allus kept meself respectable and this is 'ow I gits treated. I should a' listened ter yore Father.'

All at once she smelt the bacon burning. 'My stars!' she bellowed. 'The blasted 'ouse is a-fire, all threw yew!' She pelted into the kitchen and caught it in time. Thankful for the interruption, I crept towards the door. 'Come yew back 'ere at once, my lady! Yer not goin' anywhere terday. Yew can't be trusted, can yew? Yew c'n clean my winders instead. I'll find yew wark fer idle 'ands ter dew.'

I slunk into the kitchen, heavy-hearted. I got out the enamel bucket and polishing rags Mum kept under the sink. I pictured Arthur waiting for me on the swing-fields, his little brother beside him in the wheelbarrow. I thought of his cheeky grin and his sleek black hair and olive skin. He was different from other people. He was a diddicoy living in a caravan underneath the railway viaduct at Harford Bridges. I was madly in love with him, even though I knew he was beneath me. I was a grammar school girl now and Arthur couldn't read or write because gypsies never went to school.

'Oh Arthur, Arthur,' I wailed in my heart, as I cleaned Mother's window slowly and drearily, wringing out the cloth in the muddy water. I felt like Jeanette MacDonald in *Glamorous Night*, when her lover had disappeared the next morning, after their first night of love. No one understood how terrible it was to think of life without Arthur. I couldn't bear the thought of parting from him. He had followed me everywhere at a safe distance for over a year, pushing his brother in the barrow. Then one day we had sat together on the swings and kissed in the sports' pavilion. Arthur was strong and manly, even at thirteen. Now I would never see him again.

Last time we had met in the rain. I could see him crouching in the pavilion waiting, his jacket pulled over his head. Hearing my plimsolls pounding across the grass he had run towards me and caught my hands. We had only a few minutes together. Arthur stroked my wet hair. Neither of us said anything. Just as I was going, Arthur had taken something out of his pocket and handed it to me. It was an envelope with dirty finger marks all over it. Inside it were the rude drawings. I had giggled over them in the lavatory and hidden them in my purse. Now I had been found out. I was suspended from school because I had dared to fall in love with Arthur. Life was over! I would never know happiness again!

Mother kept me in all day that Saturday. I leaned out of the bedroom window and saw Dora being turned away from our door. 'No, she's doin' some jobs fer me. She's not goin' ter Saturday mornin' pick'shers this week.'

That night I sobbed myself to sleep. I hated everyone in the whole world. It was two days before Mum let me out again, then she sat down with a pen and ink and wrote a letter to the school.

Dear Miss Trumpington,
I got your letter. I am surprised at the way you treated my Audrey. She came home frightened out of her life, all over a silly little incident that has been made too much of. I know

Arthur and he is a nice boy. Audrey is a good girl and quite trustworthy. In these modern times it is no good being narrow-minded and I don't believe in treating girls the way I was treated.
Yours truly,
Mrs G. Emms

She handed the letter to me before she licked the envelope. 'Yew better read this afore it gets sent orf. Thaa's one in the eye fer that ole maid. I'm not a-toadyin' tew 'er, no fear.'

'Oh crumbs, Mum,' I said, 'she'll 'ave to take me back now, won't she?'

Mum sealed the envelope down. 'If she don't I'll be up the School Board an' make it 'ot fer 'er, an' thaa's a fack.'

What a devil I was at fourteen, mooching round the streets after dark in search of excitement.

'She's down the city agin, that Gal Audrey, all geared up in 'er best coat,' Mum said. 'There's bad blood in 'er and it will out. You see if it don't. She've got that green 'at on, an' all. I reckin she's with them Irish mawthers agin.'

Half-way down Gentleman's Walk, known in Norwich as the 'chicken run', I met two girls hanging round shop doorways, singing to themselves in the drizzling rain.

'*Impudent Barney,*
None of your blarney,
Impudent Barney O'Hay . . .'.

I couldn't catch the words, but when they got to the chorus they fell against each other laughing and rolling against the shop windows.

'Why are you laughing? What does it mean?' I asked. But they only stared at me, then shrieked again, banging each other on the back and gasping for breath. 'It means. . . . Oh no . . . we can't tell you that!' they hooted. I was mystified. 'Don't you know? Really, you don't know, do you? We know more than you know. We know, we know!' The little one had a red button nose in a pixie's face. Her old navy gaberdine mac was torn and the laces on her shoes broken. She was no more than eleven and not pretty or smart. Mum would have looked down on her.

'I'll show you then, what we're laughing at.' She pulled herself away from the other girl's grasp and sidled up to me. Then she opened her mac suddenly. All her buttons were undone and I could see her bare skin, yellowish in the dark. She grabbed my cold hands and pushed them down her neck, giggling and staggering about. It was soft and warm and I felt two small nipples sprouting. I snatched my hand away.

'That's rude,' I said.

'It's not rude at all. I just let the boys have a feel of my little kittens, that's all.' She gazed up at me with innocent blue eyes and her nose running a little bit.

'You'll get into trouble going about naked,' I snapped, 'and letting boys feel you. Where's your vest?'

'Haven't got no vests, we haven't.'

'You haven't got no proper chests either,' I said, 'not yet. You ought to see mine. I've got real whoppers.'

The older girl pulled her friend's arm. Her pointed chin stuck out at me. 'Oh come on! She's nothin' but a heathen girl. Let her alone.'

'I'm not a heathen,' I said, 'I go to church.'

'Yes, but what church?' Two strange pairs of eyes stared at me, knowing and sly, red-rimmed and inflamed like poor kids who went to the clinic when they were ailing and didn't have a panel doctor like us.

'St Julian's Church,' I said.

'Why, he's not a real saint. He's an English saint.'

'Don't show your ignorance,' I said. 'It's not a "he", it's a "she".'

'And who do you think you are? The Pope a' Rome?' They sniggered and whispered into each other's ears, mouths clamped against each other's heads. Their pointed ears stuck out through straight hair, cut short and combed down flat. My hair was curly and fluffy under my sailor hat. Mum had just washed and set it.

'I'm not the Pope,' I said, 'I'm Audrey.'

'And I'm Deirdre,' the little one said.

'How do you spell it?' I'd never heard of such a name.

'Don't know.'

'Write it down then,' I said.

'Can't write. Have a heart, I'm only eleven.'

'I could write when I was four,' I said.

'You *must* be the Pope a' Rome, then!' They started grinning and banging into each other again.

'And what's your name, then?' I asked the big one. 'Where do you live?'

'What's it to you?' Her small eyes were hard and fierce in her freckled face.

'Nothing. I don't care.'

'Well,' she said, 'I'll tell yer fer a penny.'

'What *are* you? A beggar in the streets?'

'All right, I'll tell you fer nothing. It's "nuts"!'

'What?'

'It's Philomena then, and we live at the Home.' She shifted from one foot to the other.

'What Home?'

'The Anguishes Home in Hospital Lane.' They were both quiet now, staring at my best clothes and my gauntlet gloves.

'Have you seen my photo? It's in Jerome's window,' I said. They brightened up. 'It never is!'

'Come and look.'

We pranced down Gentleman's Walk, arm in arm in the drizzle, banging into each other's hips, pretending to be Hollywood stars. We came to a halt outside a double-fronted shop window with *Jerome Studio Photographer* written up in gold letters. *Discreet portraits 1/9d. Weddings By Arrangement.* A framed enlargement of my face stood on a fancy gilt stool in the centre of the display. We all studied the chubby cheeks, fixed, glassy stare and Peter Pan collar.

'Coo-er, God save us. Jaizus, it's you.' Their noses were glued to the cold pane.

'Mr Jerome took it himself,' I said proudly, setting my face into a frozen expression like the portrait. I could just see him tripping into the studio, small and dapper with deep waves in his hair. I was sure his eyebrows had been finished off with black pencil.

'Come this way, dear.' He flicked open the curtain. 'Get up on the stool and pose.' I climbed up and perched at the top. 'No, dear, that's all wrong.' Mr Jerome walked slowly round me, his head on one side. 'Take your coat off, please.' He draped it round my shoulders, then got hold of one hand and folded it under my chin. 'Now, head to one side, resting your chin on your hand. Pull your hair down across your face a little on the left side.' He smiled and batted his eyelashes, as though he was doing the posing as well.

'Did you know you're Janet Gaynor to a T, dear?'

'Thank you,' I said. I felt uncomfortable with my feet off the floor and my tight garters. I frowned and wriggled.

'Now keep still and keep smiling, dear.'

A white light flashed in my eyes and I nearly fell off the stool.

'There we are, dear. You can get down now. They'll be ready for you tomorrow at four pm.' I had handed him my 1/9d and scuttled out quickly. I hadn't told Mum anything about it. I didn't think it would be shown off like this in Jerome's window.

The two Irish girls started giggling again. 'Lend us y'r hat and we'll get ours done as well.'

'You're welcome,' I said, 'but I'm off home now and Mum would want to know where I'd left it.'

The next morning I woke up with the croup. 'Yew brought it on yerself,' Mum snarled, 'yew left orf yore liberty bodice an' then yew went out last night and come 'oom wet, din't yer?'

'I couldn't help it if it rained, Mum.'

'Git yew back ter bed!'

She made me a baked custard and a bowl of bread and milk. We always had the same things when we were ill. Under my pillow was my exercise book. I was writing a story called 'Caverns of Horror'. It was about prehistoric monsters that no one knew existed and how the local native tribes fought them. Some of it I didn't want Mum to see. The last time she'd found a love story and was reading it out to my relations when I walked in at tea-time. That had nearly put a stop to my writing.

After my day in bed I was better. I got up early and put on my school uniform with a scarf. I free-wheeled through the gate on my bike, while the postman held it open. 'Letter for you, Gal Audrey,' he said.

'For me?' I grabbed it quickly. If Mum got her hands on it, she'd open it first. S.W.A.L.K. was written on the back. I stuffed it under my black school velour and pedalled away, late for school.

I asked to be excused and read my letter in the lavatory. I sat on the seat with my black fleecy-lined knickers round my ankles, in case anyone looked under the door.

It was definitely a man's hand, strong and firm. Whoever could it be? It was on a plain white sheet of office paper.

Dear Miss Emms,

I took the liberty of asking Mr Jerome for your address, in the strictest confidence. I fell in love with your photograph in his window. I must meet you, as soon as possible.

I work in the solicitor's office next door to Jerome's. Could you meet me outside there at seven pm on Tuesday, before I go to night-school.

All my love and best respects,
Derek Palmfield

I pulled up my knickers in a hurry, my heart thumping. I saw myself in the white wedding dress I had seen in the Bestway Pattern book: *A cool functional fishtail wedding gown, splashed with stars, with tight bodice and loose shoulders.* I pictured a tall, handsome

Ronald Colman walking beside me. Derek was bound to be at least twenty and I would soon be fifteen. I was ready to marry him.

I still had time to buy a new hat before I met him on Tuesday night, one with a floppy brim that tilted mysteriously over one eye, like Madeline Carroll in *I Was a Spy*. I would turn up a little late and let him get there first. He would be worried in case I wasn't coming. Perhaps he would bring a bunch of violets. I ought to take a little gold safety-pin, just in case.

'Are you the beautiful Miss Emms?' he would ask, kissing my hand. 'I never dreamt you would be so lovely. What a lucky man I am!' Arm in arm, we'd saunter down Prince of Wales' Road, like an engaged couple. 'Where would you like to have your tea?' he would ask.

'What about the Royal Hotel?' I would say. It was the swankiest place in Norwich. My Uncle Bertie was potboy in the bar there. Of course, he might let on to the family. But they'd all say Gal Audrey had struck lucky. But what about Derek's night-school class? Well, he could skip it. There were far more important things in store for him once he got to know me.

I took a long time dressing, peering into the glass. I was wearing the new hat with the brim and Auntie's court shoes. Under my oatmeal jacket was Mum's best art-silk blouse. The stars always took their jackets off when they had their tea. I dusted my cheeks with Icilma and drew a cupid's bow with my Coty Petal Pink. I crept out without Mum noticing. I was late, but I couldn't hurry in Auntie's shoes. I was sure he would wait forever, if need be. He was my fate.

I decided to skirt round London Street and approach Jerome's via Castle Meadow. I would then get a glimpse of Derek before he saw me. As soon as I reached the end of Castle Street and turned the corner, I had the sensation that something was wrong. It was connected with the figure standing outside; it was too short for Derek. I drew back and peeped out at him from the porch of Bennekomm's the hairdresser. Derek had glasses, a spotty face and a receding chin. He was nothing like Ronald Colman at all. Well, there was nothing for it, I had to make a quick decision.

I minced forward all smiles and put my hand out. 'Mr Palmfield?' He flushed and pumped my hand up and down vigorously. Close to, he was even plainer than I thought, with narrow shoulders and scanty hair. 'I came,' I said.

'Thank you, Miss Emms, thank you.'

'But I feel I ought to make it clear in advance that I'm not free to meet you again. You see, I'm spoken for, in fact, Mr Palmfield, I'm getting married soon.' I smiled into his face, fluttering my eyelashes. I'd seen Norma Shearer do it so often.

He looked so stricken that I was sorry for a moment. I thought he might break down and cry. 'Oh Miss Emms, if only I'd known. I had no idea.'

'I think you'll realise,' I said, 'in my position, I can't stand here talking. I may be seen by my fiancé.'

'Of course, naturally, I quite understand. Goodbye, Miss Emms, if only we. . . .'

I walked away quickly before he could finish his sentence. I didn't turn round until I had covered the ground between me and Gentleman's Walk. At the end of the street, I spotted two small silent figures standing in a shop doorway. I ran up to them, the brim of my hat flopping up and down.

'Hello you two, it's me. Don't you remember?' I was so relieved to see them after my narrow escape.

They gazed at me, then burst out laughing. 'Holy Jaizus, it's the Pope-a'-Rome in his Sunday hat!' We all fell into each other's arms giggling and my hat got knocked off, but I didn't mind a bit. We set off together, arms round each other, in the rain, humming and singing:

'Impudent Barney,
None of your blarney,
Impudent Barney O'Hay!'

13
Glamour Girl

'They're gonna 'ave a Glamour Girl competition an' all. Fuu'st prize is gonna be five pound.' Dad's face was red with excitement as he told us the news about the works' dance. He rubbed his hands.

'Five pound!' Mum squealed. 'My heart alive, I'm goin' in fer that then.' Dad stopped smiling and shuffled his feet, while Mum put a newspaper over the cushion before he sat down on his armchair. He was still in his overalls straight from the factory floor.

'Thaa's more fer them young 'uns, Gladys. Yew in't czackly cut out fer that sort a' thing.' He looked embarrassed. 'Now, wot about that Gal Audrey, she'll do, wun't she?'

'Gal Audrey,' Mum barked. 'Blast! Yer got a neck, puttin' ideas inter 'er 'ead like that! Yew want ter nip that in the bud. She's unly fourteen.' Mum speared a bloater with her fork and rammed her mouth full of bread and butter.

I put down my *Picturegoer*. 'I wun't mind goin' in fer it, Mum, provided I 'ad a long frock ter go in.' I had been studying Miss Janet Gaynor's costumes by Sasha, the famous Hollywood *haute couture*, '*alluring, without being too daring, but with that dash of finesse only the great designers achieve*'.

My brother got up and minced round the living-room. 'I'm a beauty queen, I am,' he sniggered, and fell over the cat.

Mum was speechless, her mouth full of bloater, her eyes bulging. 'Long frocks at yore age! Don't yew come it, yew brassy 'uzzy. I 'ave ter stint meself ter pay fer yore blummin' school unie-form. Yer not 'avin' no long frocks.'

I stamped upstairs and stood glaring at myself in the looking-glass. Then I threw my dog-eared story book with the milk-stained cover across the bedroom. I wanted to be grown up *now*! I combed my hair over one eye and tied Mum's pink georgette scarf round my neck, letting the ends trail over my shoulder. Then I went slowly down again, my hand on one hip.

''Oo said yew could 'ave that pink scarf on? And wot about that damn washing-up?' Mum scowled.

'Oh Mum,' I pleaded, 'yew 'aven't seen me with my hair like this. Wot do you think of it? Wot about me for glamour girl, eh?' I turned sideways, showing off my perfect profile.

'Snotty-nosed kids should be seen an' not 'eard. Now git that scarf orf an' git them tea-things done, dew yew'll git a clout right quick.'

The whole kitchen reeked of bloaters, even the curtains, and the sink was stacked with greasy plates. I pushed my hair out of my eyes and started on it – all my lovely plans down the drain.

Dad came home with the tickets the following dinner-time. He held out the programme. At the top it said, *Glamour Girl Contest, to be judged by Sir Geoffrey Colman, our much-loved Managing Director.*

'Oh Mum, be a sport! Let me go in for it! I c'd buy myself a new bike with that money, couldn't I?'

'Stop puttin' yore parts on! Yew give me the 'ump. I'm all on thorns. Yew never could take no fer an answer.'

'Hey look out, Uncle Sid's a-comin',' my brother bawled, ''e's brought us a rabbit, an' all.'

Uncle Sid got off his bike, a dead rabbit slung across one shoulder. Mum rushed out to meet him. 'My stars, yew in't bin a-rabbitin' agin, 'ave yew, Boy Sid? Come yew on in wi' that.'

She patted her Marcel wave, staring deep into the glass on the mantelpiece and giggling. Sid was married to Mum's youngest sister. He was nice-looking and tall, with shiny black hair and red lips. He did a bit of poaching and backed horses whenever he got hold of any money. He was always cheerful and joky. He dumped the rabbit on the draining board. Its throat was cut open like a raw red mouth. Dried blood was stuck to the fur round the wound. ''Alf-a-crown I'll charge yer. I'll be lenient with yer, seein' as 'ow I likes yer.' He grabbed Mum round the waist and waltzed her round the living-room, his beady black eyes gleaming. Mum tried to wriggle free, red in the face. She looked delighted.

''Ere, stop it, Sid! Put me down double quick. Charlie's in the shed a-feedin' them pullets. If 'e catch me larkin' about 'e'll go bizerk, like enough.'

Sid dropped to his knees on the coconut matting and dashed his hand across his eyes. 'Say you'll ditch ole Charlie an' elope wi' me. Yew know I're got night starvation over yew, Gal Gladys.'

Mum fell back on the couch, her fat legs in the air, laughing and puffing. 'Right yew are, Valentino. I'm full a' them tricks, s'long's I don't 'ave ter pay yew no 'alf-crowns ter'day, 'cause I in't got nothin' in me purse till pay day. 'Sides, I'll tell yer another thing,' she confided, with a funny look in my direction, 'that Gal Audrey want ter go in fer the Glamour Girl competition down the firm an' I're got ter buy 'er a long frock ter go in.'

'Oh Mum,' I whispered, overcome, hardly able to speak.

'A-course, I say she's too young, a little minnifer like 'er, but Charlie reckon she c'd pass fer sixteen, so it don't matter, I s'puz.'

Sid winked at me. 'Well, she's a nice little bit a' stuff. I'd chance me arm on 'er winnin' outright any day.'

'Oh Uncle Sid, yew don't mean it.' I whirled round in front of him in my ankle socks and black gymslip, my hair flying out.

'Blast gal, why ever not, yer got the looks. In't I allus said so?'

'Steady on,' my brother yelled, 'Dad's a-comin'.'

Uncle Sid scrambled to his feet. 'Git us a cup a' tea Gladdy, an' I'll overlook the 'alf-a-crown. Yew c'n settle up on Friday.'

Friday was when Mum met me out of school and we traipsed up the Co-op maids' department.

I took the initiative. 'I'd like something in black satin, cut on the cross round the hips and a low neck.'

Mum looked scandalised. 'Yew brazen 'ussy! The very idea! Black satin, indeed. They'll think yer no class. Fourteen years of age an' she talk like an ole woman. Now, what she want is something in voile with a nice Peter Pan collar and puff sleeves.'

The assistant unhooked a yellow taffeta from the rail. 'We've got a very pretty dress just come in today. It's quite reasonable an' all.' I pulled it on quickly and stood back to admire myself. It had a full skirt with a gold belt and a pretty cape collar.

'It don't 'alf show yer figger orf, Gal Audrey. I don't know what yer Father'll say.'

Mum held the dress up in front of Dad when we got home. 'Thirty-seven an' six it was. Yew'll 'ave ter go 'alves wi' me, Charlie.'

'Thirty-seven an' six!' Dad gasped. 'They must 'ave sucked yew in wi' that. Why, thaa's as much as I earn in a week.' Baffled, he went slowly upstairs to get the money. We heard the wardrobe door click. He kept his savings in a blue envelope underneath his best trilby. He came down and handed Mum a pound, folded up the rest and put it back. 'If she win, I'll 'ave that pound back, dew there wun't be no 'oliday money this year.' He was very serious.

'Oh dry up,' Mum pulled a face behind his back. ''E's that blummin' mean, 'e grudge 'is own shit.'

Half Norwich was packed into the Agricultural Hall that night. The noise was deafening, the lights blinding. I carried my gold slippers in a brown paper bag. No one could see my dress. I had my gaberdine mac on and the skirt was tucked up with an elastic band. The girls in the cloakroom ignored me; they all worked in the factory and I was a stranger. I didn't class myself with them anyway; they didn't have any brains. I hung up my mac and pulled my skirt down. I was the only one in a long frock. Mum had brushed my hair into a mass of shining ringlets with a kiss-curl in the front, like Gracie Fields. She'd pinned Grandma's Mizpah brooch on my collar. It had a gold snake on it for luck.

It was stifling on the dance floor and you couldn't breathe for the smoke. People were spilling beer all over the floor and there was a peculiar smell of old clothes and moth balls. The band struck up with, 'Yes, we have no bananas.' Everyone joined in. They all knew the words, the walls shook. I looked round and saw Uncle Sid out in the middle, half squiffy and doing the shimmy with Mum's pink scarf tied round his writhing stomach.

Just then I saw a hand waving. It was my Auntie Hetty decked out in beach pyjamas with long diamanté ear-rings. She looked a sight. My two cousins clung to her side in their baggy, short-sleeved dresses, arms dangling like pink sausages.

Mum sidled up to me beaming: ''Ave yew seen yer Aunt Hetty in them beach trousers wot she're got on? She don't 'alf look mannish. She reckin they're all the go.' They did up down the side with big tortoiseshell buttons that seemed about to pop off.

'They don't fit her properly,' I said.

'They fit where they touches,' Mum grinned. She was smart in her dress with the fan-pleated skirt and keyhole neckline and Dad was wearing a shiny silk tie. Some of the old employees who'd been pensioned off a long while wore 'We're Happy' paper hats with long faces underneath. Then the band struck up with the 'Hokey Cokey' and everyone cheered up.

'Come on yew lot!' Mum bawled, running off. I saw her a few minutes later between Dad and Uncle Sid throwing her short legs up and showing off her suspenders.

> *'Yew put y'r left foot in an' y'r left foot out,*
> *Yer left foot in an' yew shake it all about.*
> *Yew dew the Hokey Cokey an' yew turn around.*
> *That's what it's all about.'*

They nearly raised the roof; a great line of people clasping each other's waists tottering forward like some great centipede across the hall.

'The ladies for the Glamour Girl contest are requested to come up on the stage please,' a short stout man dressed as John Bull shouted above the din. He had a Union Jack waistcoat and a stove-pipe hat made out of cardboard. Sweat poured down his fat cheeks. Then I saw his dog collar and realised it was the vicar of St Saviour's.

About twenty-five girls were straggling along towards the stage, elbowed and jostled by their eager relatives. I stalked to the head of the queue in my gold slippers, my yellow skirt swirling round my ankles, weighing up their chances against me. Some had crooked teeth, or skimpy hair, or else they had blotchy complexions and big feet. None of them carried themselves properly. I decided I was the best one.

John Bull was shaking hands with a tall spruce man in evening dress. He had a thin, clever face with twinkling eyes. 'We are pleased to welcome Sir Geoffrey, our beloved managing director.'

Sir Geoffrey bowed to everyone. 'Most happy to be here,' he said in a high fluting voice. The crowd cheered, stamped and clapped.

Mum appeared from nowhere standing next to me. 'Thaa's Sir Colman,' she whispered confidentially, ''e's gonna be the judge. 'E must know wot 'e's a-doin', or 'e wouldn't be a sir, would 'e?'

'Pray silence, one and all.'

A hush followed, while everyone concentrated on looking at us. One by one the girls shuffled across the stage shamefaced. When it came to my turn I suddenly realised I was the spitting image of Deanna Durbin in *A Hundred Men and a Girl*. I walked forward, hips swaying, my chin in the air and a challenging smile on my lips.

Yelling and cheering, Uncle Sid and all his cronies surged forward. 'Go on, Gal Audrey! You're the one.' My Grandad was waving his stick, his blue eyes wet and shining. I waved back, forgetting for the moment who I was. We each shook hands with Sir Geoffrey and said our names. His hand felt limp and bony, nothing like a proper person's hand. He must be weak because he never did any hard work. He picked out three girls besides me. They stared at each other, then tried to put on a friendly smile as they paraded one by one across the stage. Sir Geoffrey pretended to hold up a pair of opera glasses to get a better view. Then he scratched his head and stroked his long chin. The audience giggled and nudged each other.

The four of us disappeared into the wings in single file and stood watching anxiously. I undid my sash and tied it up again even tighter and patted my face with my handkerchief, in case it was shiny. Then I heard my name: 'Would Miss Audrey Emms please step forward on to the stage.' My heart thumped and I held myself rigid for a moment, then fluttered gracefully on to the stage.

'I have pleasure in announcing that the winner of our Glamour Girl contest is Miss Audrey Emms.' The cheering and shouting roared out, while Sir Geoffrey handed me an envelope. I curtsied very low, then John Bull leaned forward and kissed me on the forehead. It was more like a blow, but I stood my ground, my smile still in place. I saw a large silver bowl engraved with the words *Colman's Mustard* being held up and then handed to me. I put out both hands to receive it. An angry little man in a Fair Isle pullover and plus-fours rushed out with a camera, and took a photograph for the work's magazine. 'Stand still, miss,' he hissed, 'and hold that bowl up as high as you can.'

It was all over. I swished off the stage in triumph, everyone applauding, and walked straight into the arms of Uncle Sid. Dad was standing next to him. 'Good on yer, gal,' Dad said in a strangled voice, almost as though he was going to cry. I wrapped my arms round his head and kissed him.

'Wot d'ye think of 'er then, Charlie? She's a gal to be proud on, in't she?' It was Dad's mate, Mr Bobbin. Dad blew his nose. 'I'll second that, borr,' said Uncle Sid. I opened the envelope and found the five pound note inside. I unfolded it and held it up. It was a lot of money all at once. Just then I saw Mum pushing her way through the crowd, elbowing people aside. She looked hot and bothered.

'Come on, Gal Audrey, I'll take charge a' that five poun' noo't in case yew lose it.' She grabbed the money and thrust it down the front of her dress. 'I don't mind a cherry brandy out a' this, seein' as 'ow it were me that bought the frock that won it.' She ignored the fact that I was inside the frock that did the trick. 'Blast, Charlie, look at that lovely bowl wot she're got! Did yer ever see anything like it? It'll look a treat on the sideboard, wun't it?' She held it up, turning it round so that it shone in the lights of the stage.

'It's a silver chalice,' I said.

Mum's mouth fell open. 'She's gorn and swallered the dictionary agin, Charlie.'

I put my mac on and stuffed my long skirt inside my knickers, then I changed into my black lace-ups ready to go home. They were all waiting outside getting drenched. We walked along King Street together in one big crowd singing 'All By Yourself in the Moonlight'. Uncle Sid put my silver bowl upside down on his head to keep the rain off. 'I'll never git over seein' yew on that stage, Gal Audrey. I thought yew was Deanna Durbin in that yaller dress.'

I smiled mysteriously. 'Oh Uncle Sid, yew don't 'alf lay it on.' But I marvelled at how he knew my secret.

14
None but the Brave

'Come yew on together, we're all goin' to see Rin Tin Tin, the wonder dog.' Mum started putting nuts and apples into a brown paper bag to eat at the pictures.

'Rin Tin Tin!' Dad threw down his *Sunday Pictorial*. It was Monday, but he was catching up on Pip, Squeak and Wilfred. 'I don't want ter see no pictures about damn dawgs.'

Mum stuck her jaw out at him. 'Git yer things on. The big picture starts at seven.'

'I'm not bein' dictated to,' Dad defied her, sitting there in his braces, with spuds in his socks. 'Yew c'n go on yer own.'

'Wot about the money then?' Mum glared. 'We're goin' in the one an' nines. I can't bear them cheap seats yew take us in.'

'One an' nines! Wot d'ye think I am, the Aggy Kann?'

'I know wot yew are, an' ole sheeny, begrutch every penny yew spend.'

'I'm thinkin' about the 'olid'ys in't I?' He fumbled in his top pocket with yellow-stained fingers. Out came a fag end, two long screws and half a pencil. He stuck it behind his ear and dug into his other pocket.

'Yew in't bin through my blasted pockets, 'ave yew?' he snorted. 'I should 'ave 'ad a 'alf-a-crown.'

'Bin through yer blummin' pockets? May God strike me dead if I 'ave ever done sich a thing,' Mum bawled, rolling her eyes up like a saint. 'Yer utterly bad to even think on it.'

Dad blinked and climbed down. 'Well, I din't mean nothin' by it, did I? 'Ere y'are.' He threw down the half-crown, which he'd kept hidden in his inside pocket.

'Come on, Gal Audrey, where's my Kissprufe Lipstick gone to?' Mum jammed her hat on. It had a double bow at the front that looked like a propellor. With her gunmetal shoes on as well she looked more like a zeppelin as she zoomed out of the back door. 'I dunno when we'll git 'ome,' she called out. But Dad had his nose in the *Pictorial* again.

'Put yore 'at on at once,' Mum snapped.

'Oh Mum, do I have to? I hate my school hat. Why can't I wear one of yours?'

''Ow am I goin' ter git yew in fer 'alf-price in one a' my 'ats, I ask yew? They'll ask ter see y'r birth cert-stifficate an' that'll say yore going on fifteen, won't it?'

'Cousin Vi'let'll let me in half-price,' I grumbled, 'she always has done.'

'Yis, but wot about if that other one's on duty? 'Er with the gammy leg an' the big body. She were suspicious last time, wun't she?'

I put on my school hat and sulked all the way. I knew Tony would be in the back row waiting for me and Mum to walk in. Then he would sidle up to us and sit next to me. Mum never noticed anything once she was concentrating on the picture and eating things.

As soon as we arrived, I whipped off my hat. Cousin Violet stood there with her torch in the foyer of the Theatre de Luxe. The 'The-etter de Loo', as it was known, was the smallest picture palace in Norwich. It had an upstairs and a downstairs and a glass front door. It always smelt of mice and you could get fleas off the seats if you weren't careful.

'Evenin' Gladdy, 'ello Gal Audrey. My word, she's gittin' a big gal now!' Cousin Violet had a short maroon uniform with a stand-up collar and brass buttons down the front. It was topped off by a red pillbox hat with elastic under the chin.

''Ow's yerself, Vi'let?' Mum asked.

'Well, I don't like this damn weather. I git ser much phlegm. I 'ave ter keep on corfin' it up an' they can't 'ear the talkin' on the picture.'

Mum paid for the tickets; it was half-price for me. 'Why ever don't yew wrap some a' that Thermogene waddin' round yer chest and git some Scots Emulsion, that'll cut the phlegm.'

'I in't got no money fer that sort a' caper, Gladdy. Pictures aren't the draw wot they used ter be. Me an' Wally's on our beam ends.'

'Bodily 'ealth is what yew got ter look at, Vi'let. Yew never did 'ave a strong constitution.'

Violet shook her head sadly and her torch trembled as she showed us to the seats. 'I know, Gladys,' she said, 'I'd be better orf dead, but I cuun't afford the funeral.'

'She even look like a dead body,' Mum whispered as she flopped down. Violet had a chalk-white face, but it didn't matter much, being an usherette and working in the dark. Mum flung her coat over the seats in front and stuck her handbag on the next seat. People craned their necks to look round her, muttering insults.

'Give us the bag, Gal Audrey,' she hissed. I handed it to her, swivelling round to look for Tony. 'Course, yer Cousin Vi'let's never 'ad no kids on account of 'er trouble,' Mum droned on, chewing at the same time. 'It's 'anded down from one generation tew another, yer see.'

'What is, Mum?'

'Why, the sins a' the fathers. It's in yer Father's fam'ly and it's in 'er an' all. Eats up yer lungs and stops yer breathin'. They're a pore ole lot, that fam'ly. They diddled me inta' 'avin' yer Father. I never knew 'e was tainted.' Mum sighed with self-pity. 'I could a' married that Billie Dyke 'oo's yer father's foreman now. 'E 'ad a damn sight more gumption.'

I wished she would dry up. The picture had just started and Rin Tin Tin was pelting along beside a railway track, trying to stop the train. An upturned pram with a baby girl inside it lay across the rails. Rin Tin Tin sped along barking, but the engine driver was mopping his face and didn't notice him.

My heart beat quickly; I couldn't bear to look. Someone clutched my hand in the dark. Tony was in the next seat. I could see his manly profile in the dark.

Mum bit into her apple and sucked up the juice. 'That child 'asn't got an earthly.' She sounded as though she was looking forward to seeing the baby splattered all over the tracks. Tony pushed his thigh hard against mine and I pushed back, a thrill going through me.

Just then a big blot appeared in the corner of the screen which gradually filled up the whole picture. It had got overheated. The lights went up. Suddenly everything looked dingy and tattered. The hobbledehoys in the front started kicking the seats with their boots. Tony looked the other way and pretended he didn't know me, in case Mum twigged.

The torn red curtains swished together and the stage opened up in the middle, as Cousin Violet's husband Wally came up playing the organ, elbows up in the air and head bobbing at the audience.

The boots rang out again as the boys shouted: 'Give's our money back!' Wally stopped playing and scratched his bald head.

Cousin Violet staggered out from the wings, putting her arms up in the air as though she was taking off. 'Pray silence, one and all. Please keep your seats. The programme will recommence in a few minutes.' She signalled to Wally and he struck up with 'Little

Dolly Daydream', while the curtains changed colour, fading to rose-pink, then purple. The film had started again behind him.

Then the lights went off and the curtains opened. Tony grabbed my hand again. I couldn't breathe for excitement. I remembered our first meeting at the swimming baths. My strap broke and I went right under. Tony had dived in and come up underneath me, banging against my bare chest. I shrieked and the attendant thought I was drowning. He jumped in as well and started life-saving me, trying to turn me over on my back. I kicked him as hard as I could in the crotch and he sank. Then I swam down the shallow end and ran straight into my cabin. I was fagged out. Between the two of them they'd practically drowned me. I changed and went round to the cycle shed to get my bike, my hair in rats' tails, my blouse sticking to me.

Tony had been standing there waiting for me, with his little sister in a pushchair. She was sucking on a glass feeding bottle.

'I didn't mean to hurt yew,' he said, ruffling his black curls with his strong fingers, 'but I thought yew was goin' under.'

'Goin' under! No fear!' I snapped. 'I've got my bronze.' I stared at his sister. 'How old is she?'

'Three.' Tony grinned. He had a snub nose and slanting eyebrows.

'She's too old for that bottle. Why don't you get her a dummy?'

'She bites them right through,' Tony said.

'Can she talk?'

'She can do,' Tony sounded doubtful.

'She's not too forward, is she? I was at school when I was her age.'

'We haven't got any schools at Dickleburgh.'

'Dickleburgh,' I said, 'never heard of it.' I got on my bike and my skirt flared out, showing my legs. Tony goggled at me. 'Seen enough?' I grinned.

'Can I see you Saturday?' He'd asked straightaway. But in a nice humble way.

'You're quick off the mark for a country bumpkin.'

'I'll be on the Cattle Market bullick-whoppin' a-Saturday. Can you meet me in the Drover's Arms?'

The very idea of me walking into a pub! Mum would go scatty. 'Don't count on it,' I called over my shoulder, 'but you can order me a Manhattan, if you like.' All the stars drank Manhattans, but so far I hadn't tried one, or any other cocktail. But that night I'd thought about Tony in bed and the future seemed very rosy.

Now he was sitting beside me, drawing little circles with his finger in the palm of my hand. We were glued together. Just then, his little sister woke up and fell off her seat on the other side of Tony. She screamed at the top of her voice with shock. 'Bugger it,' Tony barked as he reached down and pulled her back up again. 'Shut your kisser, or you'll get my fist!'

The way he spoke amazed me, it was so rough. Mum turned round and gave him a look. 'Keep yore voice down, little gal, or I'll report you.'

I took my hand away and pulled my Gor-ray skirt down to my ankles just as Rin Tin Tin rushed at the baby, clutched her dress between his teeth and leapt out of the way of the oncoming train. Then a vicar appeared in a dog collar, grabbed the baby and took her away from Rin Tin Tin. He watched them go, tears squeezing out of his eyes. Then he loped off with his tail between his legs.

'I don't think much a' that,' Mum snorted. 'It's too far-fetched. Gi'mme one a' your liquorish comfits, Gal Audrey. I 'ope the next one's a laughin' picture.' She frowned at Tony when the lights went up. I knew she was disappointed no one had got killed. Tony lit up a Kensitas and glared back. He was trying to sprout a moustache and it made him look a bit scruffy.

'Come yew over on the other side a' me, Gal Audrey,' Mum whispered. I clambered across, her big knees sticking into me. 'Hold yew hard,' she shouted, 'yore blummin' blouse is all ondone. How'd it get like that, eh?'

'Shut up, Mum, people will hear you. It's only the buttons being a bit too tight.'

'You're gittin' a figger on yew,' Mum said. 'I'm takin' yew up the Co-op and gittin' yew fitted fer a proper foundation garment.'

Just then a cranking noise started and the floor shook. It was Wally coming up again on the organ. He bowed low and said: 'By special request from a certain young man, called Tony, for his sweetheart, who shall be nameless, I would like to play that lovely song entitled, "When We Are Married!" '

'Oh Tony!' I thought, turning to catch his eye, it was unbearably romantic. Grinning, he winked back at me. I listened to the music with my eyes closed, picturing the two of us at the altar. Tony in his new Harris tweed jacket and me in white satin with a diamond tiara. If we lived in India or China, we could be married tomorrow. Girls there were betrothed and married before they were even thirteen years old.

Violet trundled down the aisle with a tray of ices strapped round her thin shoulders, coughing with a deep baying note.

'Listen to 'er corf,' Mum whispered, 'she'll soon be under the ground. 'Ere's tuppence, git us an Eldorado.'

I licked my wafer slowly. ''Urry yew up,' Mum said, 'I want a pittle. Leave your clo'es on the seat, in case someone nick our place.'

The toilet was out of order, but Mum forced the door open with her shoulder. I fluffed out my hair and waited.

When we got back Cousin Violet was spraying the place out with Flit and coughing worse than ever. Tony watched me sit down, his lips puckered in a kiss.

Mum shrieked out: 'Where's my 'andbag gone to? I left it under this seat and it's not 'ere now.' I turned round quickly and spotted a boy scrambling underneath the seats.

'Look out,' I shouted, 'he's pinched Mum's handbag.'

Tony bounded up the aisle, caught hold of the boy and brought him down. The bag flew open, spilling everything. 'Oh Gal Audrey, I'm gonna be taken bad. Git me a drop a' brandy orf a' Cousin Violet, quick, an' put them things back in my bag. Oh, 'ow I wish I'd never come 'ere!'

I didn't know what to do first. Tony was holding down the boy, who was fighting and kicking, red in the face. The others were crowding round the two of them, yelling the odds. Violet was smashing at Tony with the Flit spray. I gripped her puny shoulders: 'Violet, Violet, Mum's taken bad. Get the brandy! Please.'

'Oh my God, your pore Mother! She may go before I do, after all.' She let go of Tony and ran for the bottle. I got down and began collecting Mum's things. There was a Lady Jayne slumber net, a phial of scented breath tablets, a lucky pixie, a tube of Zam Buk, two pieces of chocolate and a snap of Mum and Billie Dyke on the beach. Mum was in a black wool bathing costume with long legs and a rubber helmet pulled down over her eyebrows.

I closed the bag and went back to where Cousin Violet was forcing something down Mum's throat. She gagged and her hat fell off. It was sal volatile, not brandy. 'Git me out a' 'ere,' Mum moaned, sagging against Tony. Between us we managed to haul Mother to the nearest exit. But it was locked and we had to wait for Wally to bring the key.

Tony acted like a man. 'I'll 'elp you 'ome, missus, you can lean on me,' he said, taking Mother's full weight.

'God will reward you young man,' she whispered, pasty-faced and weak as a kitten.

'I would suggest a little sit down in the Drover's Arms, missus, it's not far from 'ere.' Tony signalled to me with his eyes.

'Good,' I mouthed at him, behind Mum's back.

Mum brightened up. In fact, by the time Tony had treated her, she was her old self again. She invited him to tea on Sunday. ''E in't 'alf a nice-lookin' young chap,' Mum whispered. 'Refined an' all.'

Tony turned up the following Sunday with a bunch of bluebells he'd picked in a field at Dickleburgh. He was wearing his Harris tweed jacket and had shaved off his moustache. He presented the flowers to Mum and she came over all girlish. She went up and changed into her tussore shirt-blouse and navy velveteen skirt. We had salmon for tea and a tin of Fussells' cream with pineapple chunks. I never had a chance to talk to Tony because Mum was at him the whole time.

'That's the last time I'm having a boy home to tea,' I told my brother. 'You'd think he was Mum's young man.'

15
Boy Crazy

At six o'clock in the morning I crept down carrying my new red shoes. I heard Mum turn over as the stairs creaked. I stood still until she started snoring again. I shivered in my thin black jumper; the one Mrs Thickthorn next door had handed on to me. Mum didn't hold with it because it showed my figure off. But I had a good reason for wearing it that day.

'That damn thing don't suit yer!' she frowned. 'Makes yer look pasty-faced. 'Sides that, unly them ole tarts go about in black, not decent gals.'

I wheeled my bike quietly till I was clear of the gate, then I pedalled quickly to the end of the street. Tony cycled up and down on his racer, raring to go, his black wavy hair shining with Brylcreem. His teeth were brilliant white as he smiled at me.

''Ello, Gal Audrey, I thought you'd chickened out due to the rain.' His brown eyes brightened as he glanced at my black jumper.

'Rain?' I said, looking at the sky. 'I didn't notice it.'

'Look out,' he warned. A herd of shorthorns charged us, heading for the cattle market. The drover cracked their rumps with his whopping-stick shouting 'Whoa! Whoa!' He grinned and touched his cap as I cycled up the path. The empty streets were noisy with lowing and with barking dogs. Then they were gone.

We cycled on. The thrill of it made my stomach feel all strung up. 'Thaa's a rare smart jumper yer got on.' Tony stared into my eyes, our front wheels nearly touched. I felt almost sick. I must be empty, I thought.

'I don't mind it,' I said casually, patting my hair.

'Did you get your breakfast?' I asked.

'Breakfast? No fear, I'm in training for the time trials at Wicklewood on Saturday. Yew comin' ter watch?' He rolled up his sleeves, showing his muscles. I caught my breath and nearly fell off. Tony was now captain of the Norco Wheelers. It was an all-boys club at the moment and I was thinking of joining it, if they'd have me. I might even suggest it on Saturday.

'I don't mind,' I said, trying not to sound eager.

The woods were deserted at Mulbarton and we lay in the wet grass, sucking honey out of the cowslips. 'I in't 'alf struck on yew, Audrey.' Tony's voice shook. He plucked a sprig of Break-Your-Mother's-Heart and put it in my hair. I sniffed. It didn't smell very nice.

'Guess what – I got yew that present yew wanted!' Tony said.

'You didn't!' I couldn't be casual any more. I was too excited. 'Will you pay the forfeit first?'

'I don't mind,' I said. Tony forced my head back and kissed me bang on the mouth like a blow, hurting my teeth that were clenched together. He was very masterful. I wiped it away and he grabbed my hand. He pushed a ring on my finger with a beautiful white stone.

'Oh it's an opal, my birthstone! Just what I wanted, Tony.'

I couldn't believe my good luck. I was fifteen and a real woman who could get men to do exactly what she wanted. At the back of my mind was Mum's high-pitched voice: 'So thaa's wot yer bin writin' in them rude books wot yew've got hid up in that bedroom. All them disgustin' stories 'bout things no respectable gal know nothin' about. Yew've got badness ingrained in yew, my lady.'

But I didn't care. Mum didn't know I was the leading character in those romances I'd made up. She was only guessing. In future, I wouldn't let her find out anything. Why, I hadn't even started yet!

I walked in that tea-time with Tony's ring on my finger. Mum pounced straightaway. 'Where'd yer git that from? One a' them boys, I bet. Boys, boys, boys, thaa's all I ever gits when I come 'oom ter this 'ouse. They can't keep away from 'angin' round this door. Why can't yew be satisfied wi' one? Yer got that Tony, in't yer?' She chucked her moth-eaten coat on the table, the fur collar had gone all lumpy and one of the seams had split under the arm. She glared at me, her face working. Fat and ugly, she was, with her crimped-up hair, old and cracked like her shoes, giving at the seams and down at heel.

I ignored what she said. 'Why don't yew get yourself some new shoes, Mum? They don't look too cracky.'

She kicked them off. 'I likes me comfort. I wun't say thankyer fer them flashy things wot yew squash yore feet into. Gi'mme shoes I c'n splod about in. I don't trouble meself ter be in the fashion like some does. Them sloppy 'aporths wun't be able ter walk fer corns an' callouses be the time they're forty.'

It was me she meant, in my red patents with the Cuban heels. I wouldn't be able to walk. I'd be 'onsightly' through not wearing any stays. No one would want me. Jealous old cat! She was thirty-five and no one wanted *her*. That was the truth of it.

'Why shouldn't I speak to boys?' I said, defying Mother. 'Boys talk nicely to me. You never say anything nice. You're always crabbin'.' I was ready for a dust-up. I'd plucked up courage since Tony had given me the ring.

'Yew rotten little turncoat! All I've done fer yew and yew 'ave the neck ter turn round on yore own mother,' she spat out. She couldn't believe it, her Gal Audrey standing up to her. Mum always shut me up like a telescope.

'When have you ever praised me up? You never make a fuss of me. You don't care tuppence about me.' My temper made me cold and cruel inside.

Mum collapsed sideways into a chair, then, moving quickly, she hurled her shopping basket across the room with all her force. It crashed against the living-room wall, spilling everything. The Saxa salt burst open, covering the coconut matting. She took one look and let out a howl.

'Now look what you've done, yew brassy little bitch! I're bin draggin' round that market ter git things cheap,' she sobbed, 'I c'n 'ardly put one foot in front a' the other and I got 'eartburn as well. Then I gits a lambastin' from me own daughter an' all me salt wasted.'

But I couldn't stop now. 'Why can't you get things across the street at Woodses shop, like other people do round here? You traipse down there just to save three ha'pence.'

'Yew think I'm made a' money,' she roared, forgetting to cry. 'It's yew wot's keeping us pore! Posh schools and unie-forms wot yew 'ave to 'ave. Yew dare ter braze me out!' She lunged at me with her hard hands. I knew the feel of them of old.

I dodged them easily. I was young and nimble. I wasn't like her. 'Go on, lash out!' I shouted. For once, I wasn't frightened. Tony loved me. I was drunk with new-found power. Mum had always been the powerful one. But she was losing ground now.

'Defy me, would yer! Yew'll see wot I'll dew. I'll lock yer in this 'ouse. I'll sell all your clo'es an' them new shoes as well. I'll 'ave yew out a' that posh school. Yew'll clock on at the factory with yore father next week. 'E don't 'old wi' class distinctions. Thaa's why 'e wun't never gi'mme a penny extra. Ter think wot I're sacrificed fer yew.' She tore into the kitchen, while I piled up the groceries on the table and got out the brush and dustpan.

'Thaa's right,' she shrieked, 'yew sit on me, yew grind me

inter the ground. I'll go and put me 'ead in that gas-oven, yew see if I don't! I'll git out a' the way a' the lot a' yew. I'll make yew sorry.'

She wrenched open the oven door and turned the handle full on. The gas started hissing, the smell made me cough. But all she did was strike a match and set light to it. Then she slammed the door and began to get the meat ready to put in, dabbing at her face with the back of her hand, like a child.

'Open that blummin' winder,' she snapped, 'git rid a' this stink.'

I watched her without flinching. 'You can't stop me going out. I'll get out somehow,' I said.

'Yew jumped up little tart. Fifteen years old an' actin' twenty. Writin' all them sorft tales! The whool street's talkin' about yew. Jest 'cause a boy gives yer the glad eye. Yew think yew c'n depend on them? Why, they'll chuck yew over the minute they've 'ad yew an' look fer other fish ter fry. Men is all alike. Yore Father's no better than 'e should be. Look wot 'e got up tew that night down a' the King a' Prue'ssia. That'll allus rankle wi' me. Yew'll see. Git y'rself a bad name an' no decent blook'll want ter marry yer. Yew'll end up warkin' all yore life.'

I stared at her puffy face and red hands. 'You've had to work all your life, even though you did get married,' I reasoned, 'if I land a good job, I won't mind.'

'Blasted know-all! Yew'll land up on the streets an' git a disease, an' when yew 'as a child, that'll be like one a' them 'orrible things wot they put in sideshows. Yew'll git yore desserts, my lady.'

Whether she said 'desserts' or 'deserts', I couldn't tell. I was down on my knees sweeping up the salt. I gagged on the taste of it. It had gone into my mouth, but it was only my own tears I was swallowing. She watched me with a sneer dawning on her face. She'd got home with her taunts.

'Yew an' yore crocodile's tears!' she mocked.

I took no notice. She didn't know her Gal Audrey. She thought I was going to throw myself away. But she had forgotten that cruel little girl who had swung her kitten round by its tail. I would make those boys dance once I got hold of them. No one would make a fool of me – no fear. So far and no further. I'd keep them dangling on a string.

The salt had dried on Mum's cheeks, the same as on mine, leaving us both flushed. The clock chimed as we stood there weighing each other up. In quite an ordinary voice Mum said: 'Come on 'ere, Gal Audrey, look at that clock. Yew'd better set the table. I told that young Tony 'e c'd come to tea. 'E's the one yew like, in't 'e?'

'Oh Mum,' I beamed, 'can I borrow your sateen blouse with the bugle bead necklace? It's not too big if I tuck it in.'

'Please yerself,' she said, wetting her little finger and smoothing her eyebrows in the glass. 'I don't care wot yew do, s'long 's yew don't bring no disgrace on us.' She picked up the salt cellar. 'An' fill that up with some a' that salt wot yer spilt. It's a sure sign of a row.'

'That Gal Audrey'll 'ave to 'ave a proper costume,' Mum told Dad in a gloomy voice. 'She's fifteen now. She can't wear them kids' clo'es any longer. She'll want new shoes and stockin's an' all.'

'Costumes an' stockin's,' Dad said looking dazed. 'Wot dew I know about all that? Thaa's yore look-out, in't it? Yer got them Provident cheques wot yew pay in for every week, 'aven't yew?' He shrugged off the responsibility.

'Provident cheques,' Mum snapped, 'that mean yew c'n unly go ter certain shops, don't it? Yew in't got much choice then.'

'Such as us 'aven't got no money ter throw in the streets.' Dad appealed to sweet reason, but Mother didn't believe in it. Men believed in reason because they didn't know any better.

'Wot's the good a' me askin' yew anythin'? Yer got no sense,' Mum bristled.

'Well, yew asked me, din't yer?' Dad grunted.

'I might as well ask that cat, fer all yew know about things. In future I'll please meself what I dew. Git back ter yore newspaper and study wot them people up top is spoutin' about. Thaa's wot interest yew, not wot's goin' on in yer own 'ouse.'

'I s'puz yew want ter pick a row,' Dad growled, taking up his *Reynold's News*.

'I don't want no blummin' rows,' Mum screeched at him, 'yew can't even 'ave a simple argy-ment without yew reckon thaa's a row.'

They faced each other angrily. Just then someone rapped on the back door. 'Shut yew up,' Mum hissed, 'in front a' the neighbours, showin' us all up.' She changed her face to a pleasant smile as she opened the door. It was only my friend Dorcas calling for me, so Mum dropped the pretence. 'Come yew on 'ere,' she bawled at me, 'git yew orf ter school.'

I crammed my black velour hat on top of my fluffy hair and pulled on my blazer that had seen better days.

'Many happy returns, Gal Audrey.' Dorcas beamed and handed me a card.

'Oh thanks, Dorcas.' I turned, going out of the door. 'What about the costume, Mum?' I pleaded.

'Ask yore Father,' she snapped, ''e's the master.' She slammed the door behind me.

To have a proper costume, with a long skirt and a button-up jacket was the signal that you were a grown-up at last. One day you were in short frocks that were too high-waisted and no one took much notice of you. The next you were the centre of attention in a rig-out that commanded respect as an adult and a woman. I knew it and Mum knew it. But to Dad it was a mystery. He didn't know that what you wore could count. Mum was right about one thing at least.

I was transformed from a schoolgirl to a woman by a brown herringbone skirt with a kick-pleat and tailored jacket to match. Mum got me a rust hat as well with a little red eye-veil and my court shoes had rust bows on the front. Bearing in mind what Claudette Colbert wrote in my *Film Pictorial* about small people, I avoided elaborate accessories: *Little people must be dainty in every detail of their dress; open-work stockings and large gauntlets make you look 'all hands'. Exotic jewellery at throat and wrist leads to a top-heavy appearance* . . .

On Saturday morning I put on everything and paraded in the backyard. 'That Gal Audrey in't 'alf got a sway on 'er,' Mrs Thickthorn next door told Mum. 'She's the spittin' image a' Zazu Pitts in them clo'es.'

Trust her to say that! She knew as well as we did that Zazu Pitts was funny-looking. I rubbed Snowfire Jelly into my hands and put on my white crochet gloves. A boy cycled slowly past our back gate. It wasn't Tony. It was the start of a whole succession of young hopefuls. They leaned over the gate, pretending to comb their hair and stare in at the windows. They palled up with my brother, hoping to be asked in.

'What the hell's goin' on,' Dad flared, 'all them young chaps buzzin' round 'ere? I can't even git in that damn closet without bein' overlooked. That gal's too young ter start courtin', surely?'

But Mum only giggled and stared at herself in the bit of glass over the sink. 'Gal Audrey's gone boy crazy, I reckon.' She patted her hair and turned her head to see her profile. Then she went and put her best pinafore on.

''Ave yew bin ter git my order from the meat-shop, Gal Audrey?' Mum screeched. I'd forgotten all about the Sunday joint in my excitement.

'I'm just going, Mum,' I called, 'as soon as Tony gets here.'

'Tell the butcher I want a nice bit a' brisket about 'alf-a-crown, same as usual.'

I took my rust hat off and changed my shoes. After all, I couldn't go shopping for Mum looking like a star. Tony was wheeling his bike up the garden. I ran out to meet him. He got hold of my hand. 'Yew look a treat, Gal Audrey.'

We walked all the way to the butcher's without speaking, but Tony held my hand and pushed his bike with the other. As soon as I walked into the shop Bruce rushed forward to serve me. His soft fair hair fell across his forehead; his eyes were deep blue, staring into mine. I remembered Dad's words: ''E's a big boy that Bruce, fer sixteen. I seen 'im battin' on the cricket ground. 'E's got a fair drive on 'im.'

'Mum says she want a nice piece of brisket,' I said quickly, because Tony was peering through the window at us.

'I've got a nice bit 'ere,' Bruce winked and heaved a shoulder of beef on to the counter. I watched in admiration; he was so strong.

'I seen you in your 'at, Gal Audrey. You looked lovely,' he whispered.

'What hat?' I asked quickly. 'I've got several hats.'

'That red 'at. It suits you lovely.' He stared at me and brought his knife down, slicing straight into his thumb. The blood spattered the counter, mingling with the meat. You couldn't tell which was which.

'Oh Bruce,' I said, catching my breath.

'Blow me,' he said wonderingly, 'thaa's a rummun. The first time I've ever done that.'

The butcher rushed out, 'Come out a' the way, you awkward bugger. Go an' tie that finger up. I'll serve this young lady.' He smiled down at me, a big man with a black moustache like Clark Gable, almost as good-looking as his boy. The only thing that spoilt him was his big body sticking out in front.

'I've kept some drippin' fer yore Mum,' he winked, staring at my chest. 'My, yer gettin' a big girl now, Gal Audrey.'

I pretended to be shy, looking up at him under my eyelashes. 'Well, I was fifteen last week, Mr Thirkettle. And Mum's paying for me to learn shorthand and typewriting, you know.'

'Fifteen, well fancy that! You'll be able to keep the 'ome going soon, then.' He turned and glared at Tony through the window and Tony glared back. 'Why, surely that's not your boy waiting out there with that racer?' he asked.

'Certainly not,' I snapped primly.

'I bet 'e'd like to be,' he grinned. 'Still, I expect you'll chop and change a few times afore you goes and gets married. Just like I did.' He handed me the meat, wrapped up in white paper. His hand accidentally touched my chest, but I pretended not to notice. 'Tell your Mum she can pay me tonight. I 'ave to come past your 'ouse on my way 'ome. I'll look in to see her.'

I waltzed out, and Bruce rushed to open the door with bloodstains all over his apron.

As Tony escorted me home, carrying the meat on his saddle, I smiled to myself. I didn't quite know which one I liked the best now, Bruce or Tony. A daring thought came into my head. Why not try them *both*, like Ann Harding in *The Lady is Willing*? As long as they never found out.

I hummed to myself as I helped Mum to get the tea ready. I was busy making plans. I had a lot to look forward to.

16
It will all Blow Over

'Look at my conk!' Mum flopped into the armchair. She'd been to Yarmouth and her nose was bright red from sitting on the beach. Her dusty pink grosgrain frock with the godets let into the skirt was stained with vinegar from eating hot peas. Her Woolworth pearls had sagged.

'Them damn shoes 'as cut into me feet.' She kicked them across the room and they hit the wall. An angry red mark stretched across her chubby feet. 'Trouble is, I're got them 'igh insteps like Royalty. Y'r Auntie Renee's gone straight 'oom ter git Sid 'is tea, soon's we come out a' the station.'

Mum and Auntie Renee had been to Yarmouth on the excursion train to book our lodgings for the summer holiday. They always chose the hottest day of the year in June.

'Did yer git in anywhere then?' Dad barked, laying down his paper and running a yellow-stained finger round the inside of his collar.

'Roseberry Road. It's only twenty minutes' walk from the front. The 'ouse 'as got a name, "Ersanmine".'

'Sounds posh,' Dad said sharply, 'how much?'

'Twenty-three'n six for us two an' twelve'n six for the kids.'

'I'm not a kid,' I snapped, 'I'll be fifteen in October, don't forget.'

Mum rounded on me. 'Don't yew dare rear me up, Gal Audrey, flyin' in my face like that. I're bin down there in all this 'eat, jest ter please yew lot. 'Sides, yew'd pass fer twelve any day, 'specially at them prices wot we're got ter pay. Yer still at school, that mean yer still a kid.'

Dad shrugged and picked up his paper again. 'We'll be lucky if we're still 'ere by August 'olidays, judgin' by what that say 'ere. Look at this: *'ow ter protect your 'oom against enemy air raids.'*

'Trust yew ter look on the bright side. That'll all blow over, yew see if it don't.' She hummed to herself as she got the pig's fry ready for tea.

'Yer Cousin Maudie's comin' with us, Gal Audrey.'

'I don't mind,' I said. Maudie was seventeen and went out to work. She wore high heels and lipstick as well.

'I do,' my brother shouted, 'Maudie's got them funny teeth in the front an' she spit at yew when she talk.'

I ought to start packing. We still had two months to go, but my Guide motto said: *Be Prepared.* Besides, I had to get certain things into the case before Mum could check up. I had an assortment she might not agree with. A tight black satin blouse with no back to it and a crêpe de Chine sun-frock cut on the cross. It was really Auntie's old dance dress, with the fantail skirt turned up short. Then there was a pair of beach pyjamas I'd bought at the Co-op sales. Printed on the pockets was *Come up and see me sometime* and a picture of Mae West. They were a bit baggy, but would look all right belted in.

Everyone at school talked non-stop about the holidays and where they were going; posh places like Skegness and Cromer. Yarmouth was common, but I loved it. I was so used to it, like a home from home and full of life.

At last it was time to go and we set off one morning in pouring rain. We got on the Great Eastern Express 'Broadlands Queen'. It stopped at all the junctions and shunted lazily across the mud flats of Breydon Water. I got out my *David Copperfield* and pictured the houseboat where Ham had lived with Peggotty. My English mistress said I had a 'fertile imagination'. I couldn't sit still, I was too excited at the prospect of borrowing Auntie's long white rubberised mac and Mum's black goloshes. I would look exactly like Carole Lombard with her wickedly curving mouth and *svelte* alluring figure, blinded by her passion for Ronald Colman . . .

'Yew c'n spot that new Observation Tower from 'ere, Gal Audrey,' Dad said. He lit a Craven 'A'. 'An 'undred an' fifty foot tall. They say yew c'n see Norwich Cathedral from the top on it.'

Mum staggered off the train with her sailor hat on one side. Her hair was set in big flat waves underneath it. 'I'm drained of all me strength and me leg's gorn dead,' she wailed. 'It's always me that as tew bear the brunt of everythin'.'

It was her way of getting out of carrying the cases. Dad and Dennis struggled with Mum's big one tied up with a bit of rope and Maudie and I managed the two little ones between us.

'Listen, can yew 'ear it?' Maudie turned her head. We could just make out the strains of the electric organ on the Britannia Pier as Reginald Dixon struck up with 'Oh, I do like to be beside the seaside!'

Of course, it was a relief to know the pier was still there. It was always being banged into by ships in the fog and once it had been set fire to. Maudie and I started singing, ignoring Mum's complaints. Then we began giggling helplessly and falling about, as everything struck us as unbearably funny.

'Whatever are yew two golderin' at?' Mum snapped.

'Nothin',' we said.

'Ersanmine' had white palings and a gnome in the garden, but the latch on the gate was stuck. My brother hopped over and rang the bell, while we huddled together in the rain outside.

Mrs Killigrew opened her door a few inches and glared at us, as though she didn't know who we were. She was tall and skinny and her face was screwed up like someone who was angry and trying to bottle it up. She got her umbrella and opened the gate for us. 'Wipe your feet and leave all your things in the hall, please.' Her lips were drawn in, with little seams all the way round.

We dumped the cases and went into the front-room. On top of the chiffonier was a stuffed parrot under a glass dome, next to a pen-and-ink set. The lino was polished up and printed with a pattern like a red Turkey carpet. Hanging on the wall was a picture of an Indian brave with his squaw standing outside their tepes. A balloon came out of his mouth with the words: 'Home Sweet Home' written on it.

'Follow me, Mrs Emms.' Mrs Killigrew had a deep, booming voice.

We all trooped upstairs. 'This is the room, Mrs Emms. The premises must be vacated between ten and six pm. You may use the room in the evenings. Breakfast between eight and nine am.' She closed the door and left us inside.

In the corner was a wash-hand stand with a marble top and a basin and jug with big carnations on it, there was a chamber to match under the bed. The grandfather clock had stopped at twelve. Mum stared at it. 'She make yew all on thorns, that ole gal, with 'er dial like a wet week.' She peeled off her hat; the brim had flopped in the wet. 'This 'at never did sit right,' she moaned. She didn't realise it was too small for her head.

'Where am I going to sleep, Mum?' my brother demanded, searching round for another bed.

'I reckon we'll 'ave to put yew in that cupboard,' Dad joked. He pressed a button and a trestle bed came down from the wall. 'There y'are, thaa's posh, in't it?'

I pulled a curtain on one side and found another bed. 'Bags this for me and Maudie,' I said.

'Whatever 'ave yew got in 'ere, Gladys? It weigh a ton.' Dad heaved the case on to the bed and fiddled with the locks. As Mum pulled out her yellow lockknit nightdress there was a clatter. Under her clothes were tins of salmon and pineapple and Fussell's cream. A Mars Bar and a bag of short cakes fell out.

Mum cheered up and started singing: 'When It's Springtime in the Rockies,' as she eased off her 'Little X' corsets. Once she was ready, she crawled into the big four-poster with brass knobs at the corners. She scratched herself all over and groaned out loud with relief. Dad took off his collar and put the stud on the dressing-table. It was made of bone with a brass pin in the middle.

Mum was sitting up in bed eating Velveeta cheese on Jacob's cream crackers. Dad poured out a glass of stout, spilling it on the counterpane. 'Look out, Charlie,' Mum sniggered, 'if she catch yew, yew'll git twenty years fer that.'

Maudie and I were cramped up together in the single bed and Dennis was tucked up in the trestle. Before Dad could say, 'Pleasant dreams', I was fast asleep.

It was funny waking up in a strange room with the five of us in it and a stag on the wall. Mum and Dad were still snoring and Maudie had woken me grinding her teeth. I heard the foghorn out at sea, but I couldn't look through the window-panes. They were all misted over from our breath.

'Can you smell kippers, Boy Denny?' I whispered. I knew by instinct he was awake.

'I'd rather 'ave bacon an' fried bread,' he grumbled in a hoarse voice. ''Sides, I're got a sore froat.'

'I'm going out,' I said, 'as soon as I can find something to put on.' The room was full of our clothes, hanging over the bedrails and backs of chairs and doors.

I found my fawn hand-knitted jumper suit. It was warm and showed my figure off. I took Mum's pearls off the dressing-table and crept downstairs. There was a rumpus going on in the kitchen between the landlady and her husband. 'If I catch you bettin' on the horses again,' she yelled, 'I'm off!' I opened the front door without a sound and made for the prom.

I strolled through the empty streets, past the Naughty Nineties Peepshow. A notice on the whelk stall said: *Large Cockle teas with bread and butter, 9d.* The seagulls clattered and cackled, swooping on the fish-heads lying in the gutter. The sea looked almost solid, as though you could walk on it right across to Scroby Sands. Tiny waves were frothing up the beach and carrying the shingle grinding and grating like a cement mixer. Little ragged patches of bright blue were appearing on the horizon. It would be a nice day after all.

It was only seven and the doors of the Electric Picture Palace were padlocked. The poster flapping in the breeze off the sea showed Myrna Loy and William Powell. I studied the stills in the little windows. One showed Myrna Loy in a pure white fur coat and hat to match, getting into her limousine, with the chauffeur saluting her in his peaked cap. In the next one she was drinking cocktails in her state room at the Grand Hotel and William Powell was kissing her hand. Everyone was in evening dress. They changed their clothes at least three times a day in America. There didn't seem to be any ordinary people there like us, who kept the same things on all day.

I heard footsteps running behind me. My brother caught me up panting: 'Mum says you've got to come back at once, Gal Audrey, an' 'ave your breakfast, or yew'll git a good 'idin'.'

'I don't want anything.'

'Mum says it's paid for an' yew'll 'ave ter get it down yew some'ow.'

We sidled into the front-room where people were having their breakfast. Another lodger sat yawning next to me, like something the cat had dragged in. I couldn't tell if she was an old woman or a young one. Her hair was in papers and her face all dented. She wore an old floral chintz dressing-gown done up with a safety pin. Mrs Killigrew was serving off a tray in her turban and print dress. She squinted at my brother, who was bolting his Force flakes. 'Tell yore Mum it's getting cold, son.'

My plate had a silver cover on top of it. Underneath it was a square of fried bread, a half sausage and a rasher of bright pink streaky with a dollop of watery scrambled egg at the side. As soon as she was gone, I tipped it all into a teacup and put it under the table.

'That's funny,' she said, coming back with the tea, 'things walk in this house. I know I put six cups out just now.'

Just then Dad rushed in wearing his flannels and braces and looking flustered. 'Y'r Mother says she want 'ers took up there, Gal Audrey.'

I crept upstairs quietly with Mum's plate. She was in her pink directoire knickers and Pride of Youth brassiere, having a wash in the china basin. She dried her hands, grabbed the knife and fork and sat down on the edge of the bed as she was. 'I've 'ad a bad night, Gal Audrey. I 'ad ter git up twice, y'know. It were them Bile Beans wot did it.' She wolfed down her breakfast. 'This in't much cop,' she said, 'she's damn stingy wi' the butter, in't she? Paltry, I calls it.' She looked at me suspiciously. ''Ave yew 'ad yours, Gal

Audrey?' I remembered the cup under the table, wondering how I would get rid of it.

'Yes Mum,' I said, 'can I have an Eldorado when we get on the beach?'

'Yer a bit previous,' she said, gulping down her Glauber Salts. 'I'm gittin' one a' them Electric Friction Machines fer me 'eadaches,' she groaned.

''Ave yew seen that other lodger, Mum?' I sniggered, 'she look a sight.'

'Thaa's 'er daughter,' Mum said, nodding her head, 'she's an oddity, that gal. She look as though she want a good clear out an all, wi' that muddy complexion wot she're got.'

Once Mum was settled on a deck-chair reading *Glamour* and sucking Glacier Mints, with Dad stretched out on his old gaberdine raincoat, Maudie and I made for the Fun Fair. We threaded our way through the sunbathers, thick on the ground on their towels. We tripped over kids in rompers building castles and running about with spades and pails, hot and flushed with flying hair. We stopped to look at the sand-sculptor making a life-size model of General Kitchener and the Cavalry at the Battle of Omdiman. As soon as the hat came round, we sidled off. 'I'm going on the scenic, Maudie,' I said.

'You'll never, Gal Audrey.' Maudie rolled her eyes. She had done her hair in a page-boy that showed off her widow's peak. It was flat at the sides, with a big roll of hair turned under. She'd put on a skimpy sun-dress with bootlace straps and her pointed shoulder blades stuck out like little wings.

'You're trimmed up today, Maudie,' I said, 'yew remind me of Edna Best.' She was an older star.

Maudie grinned. 'I'm on the spree, aren't I?'

The scenic railway was fourpence, so we went on the Cakewalk instead for threepence. It jerked us about screaming and giggling. The fairground organ churned out *Tiger Rag* and you couldn't hear yourself speak. I lost my balance and fell straight into the arms of a tall lad with crinkly ginger hair and freckles. He held me upright until I found my feet. My white gored skirt blew up round my thighs. I was wearing my jockey cap that said on the front: 'Make Whoopee.'

'I'm sorry,' I gulped, as I lurched full against his chest.

'Well, ah'm not,' he winked. He sounded like Stanley Holloway who recited that monologue about Albert who was eaten by a lion. He must be from away. I trembled as I was squashed against his chest. His arms were like steel bands and I felt his fountain pen pressing into me.

'I like your hat,' he said, 'it suits you.' Just then it blew off and we both dived, ending up sprawling on top of each other. I was doing everything Mum had warned me not to. Gradually we were being rocked along towards the exit, but I couldn't see Maudie anywhere. As we scrambled off the platform I said: 'I've lost my Cousin Maudie.'

'That's funny,' he said, 'my pal Phillip's lost as well. I'm Leonard, by the way.'

'I'm Audrey,' I smiled up at him, as I fixed my hat at a jaunty angle. 'And what are you doing in Yarmouth?'

'We're on holiday with the Christian Youth Fellowship.'

Christian, I thought! There was nothing Christian about the way he'd squeezed my waist on the Cakewalk. 'Look out,' I said, 'here comes Maudie.' She was walking towards us armed up with a boy, her face wreathed in smiles.

'Oo'er, it's Phillip she's with.' The four of us stood there looking daft, while the crowd jostled us.

'We're going to the Milk Bar. Are you coming?'

'No, we're skint,' I said quickly, before Maudie could accept.

'The treat's on us,' Leonard said. We pranced off, all talking at once.

The waitress in the Black & White Moo Cow was dressed in a black overall with a white bow on top of her head, sticking up like two horns. She pulled down the handles behind the bar and milk foamed into our glasses, like beer.

'Have you signed the pledge?' I giggled.

He took it seriously. 'Yes, we're T.T. How about you?'

'I never touch a drop,' I said, 'I can't speak for others.' I gave Maudie a look.

'My Dad's a Minister,' Leonard said, 'that's why we're at the Temperance Hotel.'

'Oh crumbs!' I burst out. There was an awkward pause while we gulped our milk.

'We're going on the Broads tomorrow. Would you two like to come?'

Things were looking up. I knew Mum wouldn't let me go alone, but if Maudie was with me it might be different.

'An' 'oo dew yew think yew are, Lady Godiva?' Mum snorted, the following morning. I was wearing my white shorts and Auntie's strapless top. 'Yer not goin' out like that, my lady. Yew c'n see everything you've got. Put a cardigan over them arms, an' that chest.'

'Oh Mum, I'll be too hot in a cardie,' I scowled.

'Puttin' y'r parts on agin, makin' out yer 'ard done by, Gal Audrey. Look 'appy when I'm talkin' tew yer.' She appealed to Dad, togged up in his new houndstooth jacket. 'Why don't yew take 'er ter dew? Wotever I say don't make one iota a' difference ter that gal.'

Dad ignored Mum's flashing eyes for once. He held up his newspaper. 'I don't like the look a' things,' he frowned, 'I got a presentiment that somethin's comin'.

It was the same headline as before: *How to Protect Your Home from Enemy Air Raids*.

Mum snorted: 'Yew've allus got some excuse fer not doin' yore duty.'

'Maudie and me's thinkin' of goin' on the Broads, Mum. We've found out about the buses.'

Mum's face was like thunder. 'Why can't yew come on the beach with us, like the other gals do?'

Dad looked up. 'Yew'd better watch your step, Gal Audrey.'

'Oh Dad,' I wheedled, 'surely we can be free and easy on holiday.' I flashed a warning look at Maudie, in case she owned up. But she was keen as mustard to go, so she kept her mouth shut.

Leonard and Phillip were waiting in the Market Square, spruce in their Aertex shirts and khaki shorts. The bus was packed but Leonard's arm protected me from the rowdy ones. He shouldered his way through the crush and got me a seat. 'I'll sit on your lap, if you like,' I said, fluttering my lashes.

'Have you got a boy yet, Audrey?' he asked softly, as the bus careered through the country lanes.

'No,' I said, 'but I'm keeping my eyes open.' I put my arm round his neck and shifted about on his knees.

'I'd like to meet you again, Audrey,' Leonard's voice was husky.

'You'll have to move then,' I said.

'It'd be worth it,' he whispered, stroking my hair.

'Don't count on it,' I said pertly, but I could see he was smitten.

We hired a dinghy at Filby Broad for ninepence an hour. It had a bit of water in the bottom, and we baled it out. Then Leonard and Phillip pulled away strongly, showing off like mad. Sailing boats and cruisers ploughed through the water, nearly upsetting us. We screamed and clung to the boys.

We moored the boat on the island and set out to find a quiet spot to swim. Maudie and Phillip settled down on the bank to wait for us.

I got changed under my towel, wriggling into my black woollen costume with the Jantzen diver on the leg. 'Don't turn round yet,'

I called out. I was ashamed of the tuft of hair that showed up against my white thighs, spoiling my beauty.

'I'm ready now!' I slithered down the bank, with Leonard chasing behind. We dived in and swam against the current, coming up in the marshes on the other side. The little cove was just like a jungle with dock leaves, crushed bracken and moss. We flopped down in the sun.

Leonard bent forward and pressed his lips hard against mine, keeping his mouth closed. I could tell he wasn't used to it. I pulled away, but he held me down and went on kissing me. I shivered, feeling scared, then got up quickly. He lunged out and caught my ankles, bringing me down on top of him. He pulled at my costume, which was all soggy and wouldn't budge. All this time, we had hardly spoken a word.

'Stop it!' I snapped. 'What do you take me for?' But he went on tugging. I lashed out and smacked his face hard. He drew back, holding his cheek, looking hurt and confused.

'Sorry, I thought . . . well, I mean, you sat on my lap all the way . . .' he stammered in a strangled voice.

'I thought you were supposed to be a Christian,' I said, 'that's why I trusted you. I didn't expect you to be so . . . so . . . oncouth.' It was the only word I could think of.

'I've never done anything like this before.' He sat with his knees up, his head down.

'We'd better get back,' I said, pretending to be quite casual now. I liked him a lot, in spite of his taking liberties when I was defenceless. I decided I would forgive him.

Maudie and Phillip were nowhere to be seen when we got back to the boat. I looked over the side and found them lying on the bottom, arms round each other. 'Hey Maudie, are you asleep, we're goin' now.' She got up, her page-boy all wonky, and tottered up the bank, looking dazed. 'Come on,' I said, 'we'll miss the bus home.'

'We'll see you tomorrow at the Britannia pier, ten o'clock!' Maudie and I both turned and blew kisses, as we ran off. The boys waved until we were out of sight. Laughing helplessly, we ran along Roseberry Road, hand in hand.

From a distance I saw Dad waiting outside the house. I waved, but he didn't wave back. There was something funny about the way he stood there. I ran faster, letting go of Maudie's hand and came up to Dad panting. His eyes were wild.

'Whatever's happened, Dad?' I asked, out of breath. Had Mum been found dead, or what? She was always threatening it.

'We're got to git back 'ome straightaway, Gal Audrey,' he said in a hoarse voice, 'there's bin an announcement.'

'But what about, Dad? Why, we've only just come and Mum's paid, an' all.'

'Ole Chamb'lain's made a speech this mornin'. They've declared war.'

'Well, I never!' I said. Then I shut up, because Dad was crying.

17
Reaping the Benefit

'I're bin scrimpin' an' savin' all me life, so's you'll reap the benefit on it, Gal Audrey,' Mum said solemnly. 'You're goin' to learn the short'and an' typewritin'.'

'Oh Mum,' I breathed. It wasn't a complete surprise. I'd overheard the arguments she'd had with Dad. He wanted me in the factory. He never did hold with Mum's high ideas, as he called them. But Mum had won the day. It was her money that paid for me to go to Winifred Barnacle's Secretarial School when I finished at the Blyth.

I set off that first morning in my mustard frock with the keyhole neckline and my gunmetal shoes. They were the last word. I was a grown-up now, my stays and brassiere proved it, otherwise, Mum wouldn't have bought them for me. My curly hair had been clipped up the back of my neck and plastered into flat waves. It was called a shingle. I hadn't quite got used to it yet. The back of my neck felt chilly.

'All them gals at the Norwich Union 'ave got shingles,' Mum said. 'I reckon that's wot they 'ave to 'ave in offices.'

It was a relief when Miss Barnacle opened the door to me. I had been expecting someone like my headmistress; instead a pair of gentle, serious eyes smiled at me. 'Come in, Miss Emms.' It was the first time I had been called 'Miss' and my spirits soared. I could smell Flit and old carpets as I followed her down the corridor. Pegs, each marked with a cut-out of an animal, lined the walls. Beneath each coat and hat hung the owner's gas-mask in a cardboard box. 'You can hang your hat on this peg, Miss Emms.' I hung up my panama and gas-mask, straightened my kick-pleat and walked stiffly upstairs behind Miss Barnacle. I hardly dared move about too much. My stays wouldn't keep in place and kept riding up. Mum had bought them on the big side to allow for growth and my hips were too flat at the moment. My bust was all right though.

'I don't expect too much of my young ladies on the first day,'

Miss Barnacle's glance was kind and her long nose twitched, as though she expected to sneeze but managed to keep it in. She reminded me of Edna May Oliver in that W. C. Fields' picture, with her pepper-and-salt hair braided into big ear-phones, one on either side of her long narrow head.

'We type in time to the music, girls,' she explained. 'If the music stops, then you must stop as well.' She wound up the gramophone and everyone went click, click, click. But when I touched the keys of my machine, they wouldn't spring up again as they were meant to. 'The Golliwogs' Cakewalk' was a little thumping tune, very monotonous, but good for learning to type, I supposed. I stared round helplessly at the other girls. Their heads were down, typing busily. Some were in school uniform; none of them was dressed as smartly as I was. Somehow I felt more confident.

I had my eye on Miss Barnacle. Now and again she looked up and smiled at me in her gentle way. 'Well Miss Emms, how do you like the school?' she asked as I was putting on my hat to go home.

'Oh, very much, Miss Barnacle.'

'I dare say we'll make a first-class stenographer out of you, Miss Emms. You seem to learn quickly.' I glowed with pride and could have kissed her solemn face. A stenographer sounded much more important than just a shorthand-typist.

''Ow'd ye' git on, Gal Audrey?' Mum asked when I walked in. She sprinkled Sylvan soap-flakes into a bowl of hot water. 'I'll leave them tea-cloths ter soak. We'll 'ave a cup a' tea.'

'It was nice,' I said, trying to find two cups that matched in Mum's pantry.

'I 'ope I'm not throwin' that money in the street. I expect yew ter be the best one,' Mum said, glaring at me. 'If only ter spite yer Father. 'E's created enough about yew goin' there. I'll make that tea, we don't want a cup a' Audrey's Water, do we?' She slopped the water out of the tin kettle into the pot and put a saucer on top for a lid.

Mum's best cups were out, half yellow, half white, with a black line round the middle and a bunch of roses on top. She slurped her tea and thrust the empty cup at me, her blue eyes bright.

'Read my cup, Gal Audrey.'

I pored over the big dollop of brown leaves clinging to the sides of Mum's cup. She claimed I had the gift from Grandmother. It didn't matter what I told her, she would believe it. 'You're going on a train, Mum.'

'Thaa's good. Where am I going?' she beamed. 'I c'n dew with a change.'

'Yarmouth, I reckon. I can see a lot of water here. Looks as though you're winning something on the fair. I can see you carrying a big box.'

'Fancy that! I 'ope it's a new teapot, we c'n do with one. What else?'

Just then Dad came in and rescued me. He seemed excited about something. He took his cap off and mopped his forehead. 'They reckon they want me in the A.R.P. down the firm.'

'Did yew tell 'em yew couldn't go?' Mum said firmly.

'Thaa's compulsory, in't it?' Dad said.

'I thought yew said it'd all blow over,' she frowned.

'Well, it 'asn't done so far, 'ave it?'

In the days that followed I concentrated on being the best one at Miss Barnacle's. I was busy watching her as well. She was different from anyone I knew. I couldn't believe she was a proper person, like us.

'How can she be?' I asked Mum, 'she never gets in a temper, she doesn't stuff herself at dinner-time and she don't rush to get things first. Her hands are always nice and clean and she don't have no grease on her collars.'

Mum shook her head in sheer disbelief. 'My heart alive, she's a blasted rummun then. She's not 'uman.'

''Sides that,' I prattled on, 'she live all alone and she doesn't seem to mind it. She looks after her garden out the back all by herself. You should see her diggin'! Yet she never seem to have any taters, nor ladders in her stockings, neither.'

'I sh'd watch 'er,' Mum warned, wetting her finger and mopping up the cake crumbs on her plate with it. 'There's suffin' funny about 'er.'

I came to my final discovery about Miss Barnacle. I knew it would flummox Mum. 'And d'ye know, Mum, I think she trust other people.'

Mum stared at me. 'She must be a proper fule then.'

'That she isn't,' I said, 'she've got her head screwed on.'

'Do she run anyone down?' Mum asked.

'I in't heard her.'

Mum sniffed very loud: 'Then she's what you call a 'ippocrite.'

'Whatever's that, Mum?'

'Why, someone 'oo in't what they say they is.'

'Well, Mum,' I said doubtfully, 'she didn't exactly say she was anything.'

'That's it, then, in't it?' Mum crowed. 'She's a mystery. Now yew mark my words, myst'ries allus gits found out. It sometimes take a long while, but they allus do. Jest yew keep your eye on 'er, like I tell yew, an' yew'll find 'er out.'

I watched Miss Barnacle closely like Mum told me to, trying to find out her faults. I didn't realise *I* was being watched as well. By the boys. They waited for me to come out and followed me home, at a safe distance.

One tea-time when I was late, Mum was looking down the road as she drew the black-out curtains. 'I seen yew with another boy,' she accused, 'I said it afore an' I'll say it agin, you're fast.'

'Oh Mum,' I said, 'I can't help it if they keep on following me.'

'And why is that, my lady? I'll tell you why. It's 'cause you're boy-crazy an' they know it.'

'What's the harm if I go out with one, Mum? I'm nearly sixteen. Besides, I'm entitled to some pleasure.'

'Pleasure is what leads to ruin,' Mum said, 'you see if it don't.'

I changed into my green frock with the stiff petticoat underneath. The skirt stood out and rustled when I walked. I rubbed Doge Cream for Tired Skin into my cheeks and put on my Tangee lipstick. It was time to put my *Cheery Chicks* Annual in the bin and stow my doll in the cupboard under the stairs. I planned to join Prunella Stack's Health & Beauty Club.

'I'm goin' to see Dolores Del Rio on Saturday night, Mum.'

'Wot's the picture?' Mum asked.

'*Her Secret Desire*,' I giggled.

'Disgustin'!' Mum snapped. 'And who d'yew think's goin' ter take yew in ter see a picture like that? Yew don't know no one over twenty-one.'

'If you want to know, I'm going with Bruce.'

'Not that damn butcher boy?'

'And why not?' I asked.

'I dunno wot you're thinkin' about, my lady, lettin' yourself down like that! 'Sides, I thought yew 'ad a crush on that Tony?'

'I might as well have a second string, Mum. I told him to keep a nice piece of top rib for you on Saturday.'

'If I know that Bruce, 'e'll pinch that joint an' then charge me double the money. I wun't born termorrer, like yew was.'

'Oh Mum, you never give anyone their dues.' I flounced out and strolled down to Woolworths. I bought a pair of diamond ear-rings for one and sixpence and a trial size 'Vienna Mud Tub'. But on the way home the ear-rings made black marks, so I took them off again. I left the Mud Tub in the kitchen. Mum took the lid off, smelt it and threw it down the lavatory. 'I don't know why yew wants muddy-packs at your age. That stink pewtrid!' she bawled.

That night I combed Mum's hair before she went to bed, so that I could pluck out the grey ones. She shrieked each time I tugged at a hair and frightened Dad. 'It don't take much to frighten your Father,' she said scornfully. 'Men is all talk. They in't no good when it come ter standin' up ter things. They're useless when it comes ter the main things in life, like bringin' up the kids an' doin' the cookin' an' the 'ousewark. Wot good are they when someone's ill a-bed? I dunno wot we're got ter be troubled up wi' men for.'

I listened and held my tongue. She didn't like anyone contradicting her.

'Now yew hear wot I say, Gal Audrey: the sort a' 'usband yew want ter git 'old on is someone wot bring 'is pay-packet straight 'oom an' don't sluss it down of 'is gullet of a Friday night, or gamble it all away.' She gave me a fierce look, as I held up a lock of her thick, coarse hair.

'You're quite right, Mum,' I said.

'When yew gits spliced, tell 'im yew don't want no interference wi' nothin' yew dew, then yew c'n make all the arrangements ter suit yerself.'

I looked round at Father, but he'd disappeared into the kitchen to do the washing-up. 'I'll take your advice, Mum, and can I borrow your crocodile handbag on Saturday night?'

''S'long as yew keep it clean, my lady.' Mum stirred up her Andrews' and drank down the fizzing liquid. 'Where's my *Secrets*? I'll read that in bed.'

I hunted under the cushion and found her magazine. It had a picture on the cover of a soldier in a forage cap kissing a V.A.D., with a fringe underneath her head-dress. What if Tony or Bruce were called up? It would break my heart, I decided. But, of course, if they were fighter-pilots or brave paratroopers, it would be worth waiting for them.

The day came when I was presented with my Pitman's Diploma in Shorthand-Typewriting and Book-keeping. Miss Barnacle invited me to tea in her private sitting-room. It was done out in bottle green and the matching velvet curtains were tied back with gold sashes. On her piano stood a silver-framed portrait. I picked it up and saw a curly-haired young man in an old-fashioned soldier's uniform, with a dog collar round his neck. He must be a parson.

'Ah, Miss Emms, you are looking at my fiancé,' Miss Barnacle sighed, her brown eyes very sad. 'He was a padre in the Royal Norfolks. Killed at the Front.'

'What a shame, Miss Barnacle!'

'You can call me Winnie, if you like, Audrey,' she handed me a mustard-and-cress sandwich. 'I shall meet him again in heaven, I know that. That is what keeps me going.'

I walked home thoughtfully afterwards with Bruce. He was very good-looking with his broad shoulders and curly hair, but he wasn't very bright. Although I had a crush on him, I couldn't imagine myself waiting to meet him in heaven, if he happened to get killed.

'Bruce,' I said, as we parted at my garden gate, 'make sure you keep a nice bit of brisket for Mum, and I'll see you outside the Haymarket on Saturday night.'

Mum opened the door giggling. She started singing: '*The butcher boy, the butcher boy, I want to marry the butcher boy.*'

'Oh Mum, do shut up,' I snapped, 'I'm not going to marry Bruce and you know it.'

'An' 'oo d'ye think you're talkin' to, my lady? I'm yore Mother, I'll 'ave yew know. Men'll come and men'll go, but yew'll never 'ave but one mother, an' don't yew fergit it!'

'Someone 'ave sent yew a stiff letter, Gal Audrey,' my brother grinned a few mornings later. I snatched it out of his hands. The long white envelope crackled.

'I'll take charge a' that,' Mum scowled, 'I'll git ter the bottom of all these damn love letters that's bein' sent ter this 'ouse.'

I was only surprised she hadn't opened it already. She ripped it in two with her pudgy fingers and held up the letter, rent in half.

'Yew'd better read this out, my lady. I want ter know wot yew've bin up to.'

It was from the *Eastern Daily Press*.

Dear Miss Emms,
We have received your application of the 18th ult., re the situation of trainee reporter on this newspaper, at a weekly salary of seven shillings and sixpence.
Please attend for interview at this office at 9 am the 22nd inst., bringing your C.V. and references.
Yours faithfully.

It was signed with a rubber stamp. *For and on behalf of A. B. APPLEGATE.*

'Well I'm blowed,' Mum's face changed. 'Fancy that! Gal Audrey's got a job.'

'Nowhere near, Mum. I haven't got no references, have I? 'Sides, what's a C.V.?'

Mum bit into a round of Bermaline bread, then spat it out. 'I don't know 'oo-ever c'n stommick this brown bread,' she coughed, 'give me white any day. Them chickens c'n 'ave this.' She dipped her spoon into the condensed milk and licked it off. 'Take away the taste a' that damn muck.'

She glared at my half of the letter and sucked another spoonful of milk. 'C.V.? Well, that mean religion. They wants ter know what church yew attend.'

'I'll have to say St Julian's then.' It was years since I'd been there.

'That'll dew. They'll bear yew out,' Mum nodded, 'then yew c'n git them references wot they want orf a' the doctor. 'E know all about yew, don't 'ee?' Considering I hadn't seen him since I was eight!

'Can I wear your pendant, Mum?' I saw myself being interviewed under a spotlight in a revealing black dress, my only ornament Mum's purple pendant.

Mum frowned. 'I don't know as 'ow it's all that lucky, Gal Audrey. It was took orf a' yer Auntie when she passed over wi' galloping consumption, y'know.'

'I'm not that superstitious,' I said.

'Yew will be when you lose the job.'

I had to admit it wasn't easy combining glamour with efficiency. I tried on Mum's new black sombrero with my navy moiré frock, but the effect was dingy. I searched through *Mab's Weekly*, but there was nothing suitable for such an occasion. I would have to wear a hat, I'd be undressed without one. Perhaps my red beret would do? With my brown gored skirt and jacket it looked all right.

To my surprise there was no spotlight in Mr Applegate's office. It was dark and gloomy; the sandbags kept out all the light. I was early and he wasn't there. I sat in the corner and waited. A flyblown poster on his wall said: 'Tune into the Twentieth Century with Workers' Playtime'. Underneath was a photo of Bebe Daniels in a turban, with a black fringe and a white overall, sitting in front of a machine she'd obviously never seen before.

The door burst open and a short man with a bald head and bushy moustache bustled in. He was carrying a pile of letters. He looked horrified when he saw me. 'How did you get in here?' he rapped out. He put on a pair of thick glasses and stared at my legs in my American Tan lisle stockings.

'I've got an interview with Mr Applegate,' I whispered, losing my voice as I handed him the two halves of my letter and my reference from Dr Hurn.

'Mr Applegate's been called up. You'll have to see Mr Bodie. Wait here, miss.'

Mum was right. I took off the pendant straight away and stuffed it in my brown pochette.

Mr Bodie had white hair and wrinkles. His tie was spotted with grease, but he wore a gold pin and a gold watchchain. He rolled his 'r's' and spoke in a funny voice. 'Ha' ye ever-r been in thee Polis Court, Miz Emms?' he rumbled at me.

Police Court! Mr Bodie must think I was a criminal. 'No, never,' I said in a trembling voice. 'I've never had the occasion to go in one, Mr Bodie.'

'Weel, thaa'at's wheerr' ye'll be going, Miz Emms. The Guildhall Assizes. Repor'rts from the Bench. Can ye do a man's job, Miz Emms, that's what I want to knaw?'

'I can do a hundred and twenty a minute, Mr Bodie.' I handed him my Pitman's Diploma. It had only just occurred to me what he meant.

'Never'r mind, young woman. I see you've got a clee'an bee'l of health!' He tapped his teeth in the front with a paper knife and glared at the middle of my chest, where the pendant had hung. Then, without a word, he got up and stalked out. He'd changed his mind and he didn't know how to turn me down, I thought. The telephone rang a long while, then stopped. I had gone stiff all over with the worry of whether to answer it, or not.

Just then the siren started wailing, up and down. People were rushing about shouting and doors were slamming. I dived out and ran all the way down St Botolph's Street and straight into the church. I crouched down beside the font. If it got a direct hit, I would be saved. The place where babies were christened *must* be safe.

But it was only a practice alarm. In a few minutes the all-clear sounded and I trudged home through deserted streets. Mum was still in bed reading Boy Denny's *Comic Cuts* with a solemn face. The room was strewn with toffee papers. She'd forgotten all about my interview. 'Make us a cup a' tea, Gal Audrey,' she mumbled, her mouth full.

I put the kettle on and lay the pendant on the mantelpiece. A letter was pushed underneath the clock. I picked it up and found it was addressed to me. It had been opened and clumsily sealed up again. I read it with dismay. The arrangements had been changed. The letter had arrived two days earlier, according to the postmark.

Dear Miss Emms,
Re aforementioned situation.
Would you please attend for interview on Monday 25th, instead
of the 21st, due to staff indisposition.
Yours faithfully,
A. B. Applegate

I raced back upstairs, furious. 'Look at that!' I blazed at Mum,
hurling the letter across the bed at her. 'You saw me getting ready
for my interview this morning. I went to all that trouble and all the
time this letter was lying there telling me to come on a different
day!'

'Don't yew dare talk ter me like that, yew brassy 'ussy! Yew c'n
git out a' this 'ouse, double quick!' she blustered. ''Sides, I don't
'old with jobs at seven-an-six a week. I allus pictured yew at the
Norwich Union, where they git good money.'

'You won't catch me writing for any more jobs,' I said, 'I'm
finished!' I stormed out, determined never to speak to Mother
again.

I woke with a start the next morning. I heard the postman
whistling. I'd had a strange dream. I was at the Regent, and a little
ball was bouncing on the words printed on the screen, but I
couldn't sing because it was in shorthand. It wasn't Pitman's, but
something I didn't understand. I rushed downstairs and found yet
another letter from the newspaper, offering me the job. They
wanted me to start on Monday morning!

'Mum,' I said beaming, 'I got that job. Can you lend me five
shillings till I get paid?'

I went to Timothy Whites & Taylor and bought an Icilma
shampoo. At Jarrolds I bought Roget's Thesaurus. I stood outside
the newspaper office clutching my book and watched the staff
going in and out. As the door opened I peeped in and saw the
compositors at work, wearing green eyeshades like Mickey
Rooney wore in the Andy Hardy pictures.

Mum was making a carrot flan when I got home and grumbling
about the trouble of it. 'I can't git a tin a'fruit anywhere, all them
rich people 'ave bought up the lot. They saw it comin', a' course,
shortages. Thaa's more 'n yer Father did. 'E's a pratt.' I looked at
the carrot flan. It reminded me of a cow-pat, but I didn't say
anything.

I went through my Pitman's Letters of Commerce. Under
'Acceptance' it listed employment, legacy, matrimony, consign-
ments c.i.f. or f.o.b. I wrote:

Dear Sir,

. . . I beg to accept your esteemed offer of employment, with the utmost pleasure and will attend at your office on Monday.
Your obedient servant,
Audree Gladys Emms (Miss)

I decided to spell my name with two ee's. It looked much more distinguished.

That first morning I set off early with Dad, in my tailor-made costume with a white organdie blouse underneath. Dad sniffed: 'Yew got scent on, Gal Audrey?'

'*Evening in Paris*', I said, 'hope it's not too heady.'

He chuckled. 'They'll know you're comin' then.'

Mum leaned out of the bedroom window, her steel curlers jingling and her old red coat pinned up under her chin. 'Gal Audrey, 'ave that costume bin aired?' she bawled.

'Yes Mum,' I lied.

Her frown gave way to a grin. 'Fare ye well, tergether,' she called, and smashed the window down.

Dad cleared his throat, getting ready to say something. 'She's a rummun, your Mother. One minute a-cryin', the next minute a-laughin'. Yew never know where yew are with 'er.'

I linked my arm through his, as we marched down Queen's Road. 'It's how she is,' I said, 'she'll never alter, but I'll be different.'

'Yew always was, Gal Audrey.' Dad smiled and saluted me as we parted company at the crossroads and I went on to London Street.